AMWAY

Behind
the **MOTIVATIONAL**

Smoke
ORGANIZATIONS
and

Mirrors

By Ruth Carter

Backstreet Publishing
Winter Park, Florida

Published by Backstreet Publishing
127 W. Fairbanks Ave.
PMB 409
Winter Park, FL 32789-4326

Printed in the United States of America

Library of Congress Catalog Card Number: 99-61374

ISBN 0-9671070-2-4

Design by Backstreet Publishing
Cover Design and Illustration by Stampato Designs

Acknowledgments

Far too many people have helped with this project to name individually, even if they wanted their names in print:

First, my husband, whose love and support has been unwavering in spite of everything. The pioneering website authors, who dared to tell the truth and made me aware that I was not the problem. My editor and my legal advisor, whose solid work and encouragement has made a big difference. Family and friends who have forgiven us for all those years when we treated them so badly. Bob FitzPatrick, co-author of *False Profits: Seeking Financial and Spiritual Deliverance in Multi-Level Marketing and Pyramid Schemes* and Steven Hassan, author of *Combatting Cult Mind Control* for putting up with all my questions. And for all those distributors and former distributors I've been in touch with via e-mail, fax and phone who shared their thoughts, beliefs, stories and sometimes horror stories, and helped me believe that this work is necessary.

Table of Contents

ONE

It was February, and I was tired of the cold, the snow, and ice, and wood heat. I was 28 years old, living with my children, unexpectedly single. I was in shock, although I didn't know that at the time.

A neighbor called one evening. He told me that he was considering starting his own business, was going to be meeting with an associate, and wondered if I would join him and help him evaluate this business as he respected my judgment. (I was a small business owner.) I was not the slightest bit interested in his business ventures, but at this point I was totally starved for adult companionship. I agreed to meet with him.

That evening started a journey – that lasted for more years than I care to admit to – of involvement in the Amway business. I was totally involved, or **core**.* I bought the products, I held meetings and sponsored people, I went to all the functions I was **qualified** to attend. I spent a fortune on tapes, books, and other motivational and training materials. I was a single mom, and I was leaving my kids with teenage babysitters for at least one weekend every month so I could attend a **Seminar & Rally** three hundred miles away. Several nights a week I would

---

*   The first time a word is used here which has a specialized meaning within the Amway business , it will be shown in **bold** type. Please see the Glossary for a definition.

pick my kids up from the babysitter after work, drop them with a different sitter, then run out the door to show the plan, contact new prospects, or sell product. I was broke and getting broker.

My **loyalty** to the **system** brought me to the attention of my upline **Diamond**, who offered me a job in his office. I was flattered, and felt it was too good an opportunity to turn down. With stars in my eyes, I was excited about being able to rub shoulders with the **Pearls** (now changed to **Sapphires**), **Emeralds** and Diamonds in the organization.

Unfortunately, despite my starry-eyed loyalty, I had neglected to park my brain at the door. As I learned more and more about the inner workings of the business and the so-called *Diamond Lifestyle*, I became more and more disillusioned about the Amway business.

What Is It About Amway?

Few businesses have been as controversial for as many years as the Amway business. What is it about a company, headquartered in the Midwestern United States, that arouses such passionate responses? Anyone who has experienced the Amway business either loves it or detests it – there seems to be no middle ground.

On the surface, such passions appear ludicrous. It's just a company that manufactures a line of basic household and personal care products, and supplies name-brand products through a catalog. Or is it?

In the pro-Amway camp are those who claim to have developed significant wealth using the Amway **multilevel marketing** plan, or those who know someone who is successful in the business. Also in the pro-Amway camp are well-known Republican politicians, including Ronald Reagan, George Bush, Oliver North, Newt Gingrich, Woody Jenkins and Sue Myrick. Conservative Christian leaders James Dobson, and formerly Jim and Tammi Bakker have been staunchly pro-Amway, and claim friendships with Amway founders and high-level distributors. Jerry Falwell, who receives massive donations from Amway leaders, has recently issued statements on the internet, and through Amway's voice messaging system, supporting Amway against its critics. Author Charles Paul Conn, president of Lee College, a small Christian college in Cleveland, Tennessee, has written six books about the Amway business, and was a favored speaker at Amway conventions for a number of years;

and a number of entertainers and motivational speakers support the Amway business.

Rabid anti-Amway sentiment is expressed by thousands of former distributors, families and friends of distributors, and many religious leaders and liberal politicians. Since the advent of the World Wide Web and more widespread use of the internet, people around the world, many of whom are former distributors, are actively speaking up about their experiences and what they perceive as illegal or unethical aspects of the Amway business. Amway is often accused of cultlike activity, of using deceptive mind-control practices to control distributors and keep them in the system, spending their money on endless unneeded products and repetitive motivational tools.

At least 18 significant lawsuits have been filed against Amway and the highest-ranking Amway distributors. Amway has pleaded guilty to charges of customs violations against the government of Canada, and paid $25 million in fines and a $45 million settlement.[1] (*Wall Street Journal*) As of this writing, Amway is defending suits brought by Procter & Gamble of Cincinnati, Ohio which involve charges of unfair competition, fraud, and racketeering. One suit claims that the Amway business is "in reality an elaborate, illegal pyramid scheme." Additional charges include "false and misleading advertising." The suit also charges that Amway distributors are, in fact, "employees and agents of Amway," and are also "commissioned sales agents," not independent contractors, and further charges Amway with "negligent supervision" of its sales force. There have been a number of lawsuits brought by distributors and former distributors against Amway Corporation and specific Amway distributors. One recent suit involves 29 very high-level distributors, who are suing Amway and one of Amway's most successful distributors for $200 million. Another recent suit was brought by a high-level distributor against Amway and a number of other high-level distributors, seeking $50 million in compensation for lost income. There have been class action suits, and numerous individual suits. There are former distributors who claim to have lost their shirts, their marriages and their families because of the Amway business.

Amway itself claims to be a beacon of free-enterprise hope throughout the world. The company's goal, expressed by President Dick DeVos and Board Chairman Steve Van Andel, on Amway's World Wide Web site, is to be "The best business opportunity in the world."[2] (Amway, internet) According to a January, 1998 Amway Corp. publication, "Amway has succeeded for more than three decades in a highly regulated industry, because it is a proper, ethical, and honorable addition to the retail marketplace."[3] (SA4400) Amway promises wealth, opportunity and freedom for those who join and are willing to put in significant time and effort.

How do we reconcile these widely divergent views of a business? What inspires the passion about this company, which started out in 1959 selling a single organic cleaning product? What is behind the smoke and mirrors of the Amway business?

Let's look at some case histories, beginning with my own.

TWO: How I Got Started

I See The Plan

It is the dead middle of a horrible winter. In December my husband had left me and our young children to move in with another woman. I was in shock. I remember very little of that winter other than alternating rage and depression.

I lived in a nightmare of logistics. My house was heated with wood. I had an oil-fired furnace, but it was just used as emergency backup since we couldn't afford to run it full-time. My house on the hill, which during the summer showed me stunning mountain views, in the winter was difficult to get in and out of. My day started early, of course. I would take my oldest child to school and do errands or stop for groceries on the way home.

After the morning school and errand run, I brought in the firewood for the day and stacked it by the stove. Some days, of course, I had to do this more than once as I didn't have enough room to stack enough for an entire day when it got really cold. I attempted to do some work, phone clients, and so on, but I accomplished little and my business was falling away fast. I didn't want to leave my infant with anyone else. The closest member of my family lived over 150 miles away; my parents were 300 miles away, and my siblings farther than that. My long-distance phone bill skyrocketed, hitting almost $300 one month. Back in 1982, that was a lot of money to spend on long-distance calls!

After a couple of months of this logistical nightmare, I receive a call from my neighbor. He explains that he is evaluating a business. Since he has great respect for my business judgment, he wants to ask for my help in this evaluation. He can't really tell me much about it, but would like me to come and meet the person he will be associated with. Maybe I'll even see some potential for myself in the concept! I am not at all interested in helping him evaluate his business deal, but I'm sick of my own company and problems. I tell him that if his daughter will watch the children for me, I'll come.

At the appointed time, I drive to his house. As agreed, his daughter takes the kids. I'm wearing jeans, down jacket, and snowmobile boots – normal winter attire. My neighbor is wearing dress pants and a button-down shirt, with a tie that's too short. I have never seen him in anything but jeans or shorts in all the time I've known him, and certainly had no notion he even owned such a thing as a tie. Several other people are there, including one man wearing a black suit, blindingly white shirt, red tie, and enormous smile. He introduces himself to me. He is Steve Silver (not his real name, but the name we will use in this book), and begins asking me some questions about myself.

After a few minutes, when it becomes obvious that I'm the last arrival, my neighbor goes to the front of the room where a white board is set up on an easel. He introduces his "good friend" Steve Silver, who is very successful in the business that we are there to look at. Steve will tell us all about it.

Steve begins his presentation. I am confused. I had expected to meet somebody who would be talking about specific business plans with my neighbor. Instead, Steve's up there talking about dreams and goals, a "Five-Year Plan" vs. a "Forty-Year Plan." Oh, well. It would be rude to interrupt.

Steve talks about cars, homes, vacations, sending children to private school, money in the bank. Now we are all leaning forward in our seats, smiling. He talks about education, and how more education doesn't usually translate into a better lifestyle. He talks about retiring from our jobs within two to five years, and having time to spend with our families. I start paying more attention. He zips through a lot of numbers, then gives a brief history of the company that has put together this wonderful program. At the critical moment, he flips up an enormous poster of the Amway World

Headquarters in Ada, Michigan. I have no experience with Amway, so this means little to me.

When the presentation is over, my neighbor brings out refreshments: Kool-Aid or coffee in styrofoam cups, and store-bought cookies. Back then, I would have willingly agreed to be flattened by a bulldozer sooner than serve a guest in my home a cookie bought from the store. And, I wonder, where is his wife? Her car is in the driveway, so I assume she's home, but we haven't seen her all evening. Besides, it's not like her to serve this kind of food. What's going on?

But then Steve is in front of me, asking, "Do you see anything here that interests you?" He starts talking about dreams, and quickly realizes that time with my children is my hot button. He offers to give me some material to take home, material that will tell me more about this wonderful business opportunity. Well, I've been in sales for years, so I recognize the material for what it is – a reason for him to come back and talk to me two days later. I accept the material and make the appointment for him to stop by on Saturday and pick it up. I'm starting to get excited about the Amway business.

The material that Steve sends home with me includes a couple of books: *The Magic of Thinking Big* by David Schwartz, and *The Possible Dream* by Charles Paul Conn. There are also several tapes, including Rich DeVos' *Ten Points*, an *Amagram* magazine, and a few other odds and ends. Being a voracious reader, I plow through the books quickly. I'm not terribly interested in the tapes, but manage to listen to one of them before the Saturday appointment.

One of the people who attended my neighbor's meeting is an acquaintance. I speak with her, to find out what she thinks of the idea. She is upset that our neighbor did not tell her up front that it was the Amway business, and she has no plans to get involved. Smugly I think to myself, "she's really losing out on a good thing!"

The Follow Up

Saturday afternoon Steve comes by in his beat-up, rusty station wagon. I ask him why, if he is so successful with the Amway business, does he drive such a wreck of a car. He explains that because of the debt load he and his wife had been carrying before the business, he is still paying off previous obligations, but that he expects to have a new car within a few months. Then, quickly switching gears, he starts talking about my dreams and goals, my desire to be home with my children and how the Amway business will help me fulfill those dreams. He **shows the circles** again. Before he leaves, he gives me a bunch more tapes to listen to, and several new books. We agree that I will attend another get-together (he never once slips up and refers to them as "meetings") at my neighbor's house in a few days. Not only can I attend myself, but I can bring somebody if I want to! I'm so starved for adult company that I keep Steve there talking long after he should have left for his next appointment. I wonder – fleetingly – when Steve sees his own family since he's obviously got appointments stacked back-to-back all day Saturday.

The Next Step

The evening before the scheduled meeting, the neighbor who had invited me to the first meeting calls me. "Sorry," he explains, "for personal reasons I've decided not to get involved in the Amway business, but it's still a great opportunity and I would encourage you to pursue it. If you want, you can attend a get-together at the home of the person who introduced the business to me, Sally Sponsor." He gives me directions, and I arrange for his daughter to come and babysit while I go to this meeting.

I call Sally to be sure it's all right for me to come. When I arrive, she and Steve are there and the white board is already set up. Nobody else shows up. Steve decides that this is a good chance for Sally to learn to show the plan, so he stands her at the white board and has her go through the numbers. Afterwards, we sit around drinking coffee from styrofoam cups and eating store-bought cookies. Steve explains to me that the following Saturday there will be a Seminar & Rally in a city about an hour away, and that I should plan on being there.

How can I possibly go? I can't stop nursing my baby for that length of time. Steve and Sally have the solution. Steve's home is only about 20 minutes from the Seminar & Rally location. We can go there, and Sally 's daughter will come along to babysit the children. During the dinner break between the afternoon and evening sessions, I'll have plenty of time to drive to the house, nurse the baby, eat some dinner, and be back in time for the Rally. This way I can also meet Steve's wife Sarah, and she can ride with us to the Seminar as he has to take their only car to be there early to help set up. I agree, so Sally takes out her wallet and says, "you'll need a ticket. That's $6.00." I am too embarrassed to tell them that if I'd known there was an admission price I wouldn't have agreed to go. I don't even have money for the babysitter, let alone a $6.00 ticket. But I write out a check, hope it won't bounce, and trade her the check for the ticket.

Seminar & Rally

The morning of the Seminar & Rally, Sally arrives at my house, along with her daughter Susie. We put everyone in my car and drive forty minutes to Steve and Sarah's place. Their home is not impressive, to say the least. We get the children and Susie settled, along with Steve and Sarah's two children, and Sally, Sarah and I head for the Seminar.

When we arrive at the school where the Seminar & Rally is being held, Sarah disappears. Steve is greeting people at the door, and I feel incredibly special when he beams at me, shakes my hand between both of his, and says, "I'm so glad you could come!" Sally takes me around and introduces me to lots of people. Most of them have little pins on their lapels, black, red and green, silver and gold. I ask Sally what they mean, but I'm overwhelmed and it takes a while for me to realize that the folks she is introducing are all in our **upline**. Almost all the men there are wearing navy blue or black suits, white shirts, and red ties. The women are wearing dresses – not business suits, but frilly dresses. The few who are more casual, or the lone woman in pants, stick out like sore thumbs.

I am a bit surprised at the enthusiasm I see during the Seminar. None of my Chamber of Commerce, Business and Professional Womens Club, or other business meetings have prepared me for this. Each new speaker is greeted with a standing ovation and cheers and whistles. Attendees scream and shout. "Let's see who drove the furthest to get here. If you drove 30 minutes or more, stand up!" Cheering and shouting. "One hour or more!" "Two hours or more!" "Two and a half hours!" "Three hours!" "Is there anybody here from Northville? From Southtown? From East Village? From West Suburb? How about from right here in Cityville?" Then in hushed tones, "Look at that folks, only five people here from Cityville. Guess it ain't saturated!" Cheers, clapping, laughter and shouts.

Finally the speakers are introduced, a young **Emerald** couple from a neighboring state. They spend about two and a half hours teaching us how to dress, how to answer the telephone, how to **FORM**, prospect, contact, invite, show the plan, and follow up. They tell us that we're **winners** because we're here today on this beautiful Saturday afternoon. They run overtime, and I glance surreptitiously at my watch. I'm beginning to have that over-full sensation that all nursing mothers have from time to time, my body's way of saying, "go feed your baby." Finally it's over, and I grab Sally and race out to the car and back to Steve's house.

After a very hasty supper at Steve's, we return to the school for the Rally. This, I am told, is the "fun" part of the day. This is where the speakers get to tell their story. But before the story, we have an introduction, a Pledge of Allegiance, a prayer, and **pin recognition**. The Direct Distributors have changed their clothes: the men are still suited, but the ties now are dark, and the women are all wearing floor-length gowns. I watch carefully as a handful of excited distributors races up to the stage. "New 1500s! New 4000s! New Silvers!" Each is more excited than the last. With each succeeding pin level, the distributors are allowed to say more. The 1500s get to give their names. The 4000s can say their names and where they're from. The Silvers add what they do for a living. The audience is bobbing up and down like a room full of Jack-in-the-Boxes as they give one standing ovation after another. (Pin recognition levels have changed since then: now distributors are recognized at 1000, 2500, and 4000.)

The speakers are finally introduced. He has changed into a bow tie that matches his wife's evening gown. They begin their story, he says a few words then goes offstage to a standing ovation. She tells of dead-end jobs, a series of failed businesses that they thought would be their tickets to freedom. She talks about becoming involved in Koscot, a company that was found to be an illegal pyramid. Then she turns the microphone over to her husband, and he tells the Amway part of their story. He finishes with a dream session. "Imagine you're on a plane to Hawaii. . ." He talks about this trip to Hawaii, just the two of you along with a hundred or so of your closest friends in the Amway business. I am getting bored, and also struggling with the previously mentioned full feeling. I start looking at my watch. Ten minutes. . . fifteen. . . thirty. . . . He talks for *forty minutes* about this imaginary trip to Hawaii. It seems like forever. Afterwards, all of the Direct Distributors go up on stage, and everyone in the room holds hands and sings *God Bless America* while swaying back and forth to the music. I notice that the Directs all come in couples. In fact, every one of the pin awards that day goes to a couple. I ask Sally about this, and she admits that the business is predominantly couples building it together, but there are more and more singles getting involved.

As I bolt from the auditorium, I hear someone say, "wasn't that a *fantastic* dream session?"

Have a Get-Together

The next day, Steve calls. Wasn't it a great Seminar & Rally? Wasn't it a super dream session at the end? We need to plan my first get-together – which would be better for me, Tuesday night or Thursday night? I have some qualms after the Seminar & Rally, which I express to Steve. The woman of the couple who spoke is very much a quiet-spoken, "now, girls, you need to stand behind your man and support your man" type, and received much applause from the audience for this position. I have for years been active in a local women's organization and the League of Women Voters, and had helped to found a chapter of the Business and Professional Woman's Club in my community. Especially in light of my current divorce, hearing people cheer for a woman who is glorifying her subservient role to her husband is extremely irritating, but Steve pumps me up and conveys his feelings of excitement about how great my business will be. "After all," he says, "when you go Emerald, you can get up on stage and tell *your* story." I have no way of knowing at that time that what I heard at the Seminar & Rally is the only acceptable position for a woman in the Amway business. 'What do I have to lose?' I think. I won't even have to pay a sitter for this next meeting, as people will be coming to my home. All I have to do is make some phone calls. I can do that!

> At one function my husband was told to be the top dog and that he should make me roll over and wet myself. When we took that upline they said that that was a good philosophy!!![1]

I make a lot of phone calls, about 60 in all, and invite people to my get-together. Steve has already clued me in that we *never* call it a meeting, as meetings either intimidate or bore people. And I shouldn't make any refreshments, as many women are turned off by that, thinking that if they join the business they'll have to bake. I should use styrofoam cups so that cleanup is simple – we don't want anyone to feel that they have to wash a lot of dishes afterwards. I grit my teeth and buy cookies and styrofoam cups.

About eight people come to my first meeting. When Steve gives me the high sign that it's time to get started, I stand up and introduce him. He is my "good friend," he's "very successful with this business opportunity that he's going to show you" and "I know you'll be excited when you learn what we're involved with." I have known Steve, my good buddy, a long time now – over a week!

One prospect is quite excited, so Steve arranges to follow up with her and I agree to follow up with the others. Steve, of course, has given them take-home materials: *The Magic of Thinking Big, The Possible Dream, Ten Points*. After all my prospects have left, Steve says, "I have something in the car for you." He returns, wearing a big smile and carrying a large cardboard box. "I've got your kit!" he announces. Neither Steve nor Sally had asked if I wanted the kit, was ready to spend the money (about $65.00 back then), or even if I wanted to become a distributor. Unwilling to admit that I'm not ready for this step, I go along with it. We spend another hour "breaking the kit," with Steve explaining to me all the wonders of product concentration to take my mind off the size of the check I'm writing. He glosses quickly over the *Distributor Manual*. "Don't bother with that," he informs me, "it's just a lot of detail. If you have any questions, just give me or Sally a call."

I'm now an official Amway distributor. Sally has just sponsored me as her first, although I don't know it at the time. My life is a hazy blur of excitement and exhaustion.

Ashley's Story

I interviewed Ashley Wilkes, a former distributor, on April 9, 1998. Wilkes, a photographer from Sunrise, MN, has maintained a web site since early 1996, where he claims that his Amway involvement cost him his marriage. He was a distributor for about four years in the World Wide Dream Builders organization (now the International Leadership Development (ILD) organization of Jack and Rita Daughery). Here is his description of his introduction to the Amway business.

Well, I came home one day after work and my wife was walking around with earphones on and a tape recorder strapped to her waist and listening to some kind of tape, and she had this kind of demented smile on her face and a sparkle in her eyes, and I was real curious what she was listening to, so I asked her. And she said, 'you wanna listen to it?' So I put the headphones on and listened for a while to some guy speaking about a business opportunity and how great it was and everything, and I said 'What is this? And my wife said, 'oh, it's something that my friend Sylvia and I are doing together.' 'Well, what is it?' 'Well, it's a marketing opportunity.'

Well, I went on just trying to get more information from her but she was real reluctant to get more specific, and this went on for quite a while, maybe half an hour, 45 minutes. and then she said, 'World Wide.' Not one word about Amway. Finally she gave in and she said it was World Wide. And I said, 'what's World Wide?' and she said, 'well it's a service corporation.' 'Well, what's a service corporation?' Well, we went around like this and she was hemming and hawing and all this stuff, and I kept trying to get some specifics out of her she wouldn't give it to me. She finally said, 'would you come to a meeting and we'll show you what it's about?' 'No way,' I said, 'this sounds really fishy to me. How come you can't give me any straight answers?' She said, 'well, because I might not do a very good job of explaining it to you, and if you listen to people who know what they're talking about you'll be much better off.'

We had several more conversations about it. Finally she went on about World Wide a little bit longer, and I think about 30 years ago there was a discount catalog called Worldwide and I asked her if that's what it was. She said, 'well, we do offer products at a discount.' I said, 'So that's what it is? This is Worldwide, this outfit that sells products at a discount' She said 'yes,' She's still misleading me! She said 'yes!'

And apparently, and in retrospect I look back on it, and I know that her sponsors told her to do everything that she could to delay it until she could get me to a meeting. So that's what she was doing. She was doing what her upline told her to do.

. . . And she just pressured me, you know, and finally I gave in and said, 'oh, what the heck,' you know. 'What have I got to lose?'

So Rick and MaryJane Matthews came over. They were Directs at the time. They came over, and came driving up in their 1979 renovated white Mercedes, it was really nice. They got out, and they were very, very well dressed, they just looked really impressive. Sharp looking couple. They were both teachers at the time, actually, they both had teaching certificates. Mary Jane was a teacher and Rick was a high school counselor. Very intelligent, very friendly. I was impressed. I was totally thrown off by this. So they sat down and talked with me about what I was doing with my life, what my goals were, and all that stuff. They were really nice, I really liked them. So then they asked me if I'd be interested in looking at the business opportunity, at Amway, because they said that it had changed a lot, and it wasn't selling soap door to door and all this stuff. And I said yeah, I'd be interested in taking a look at it . You know, what do I have to lose?[2]

Ashley Sees the Plan

The Matthews told Ashley to invite everyone he knew to his home for an initial meeting, that it was important to get as many people as possible to his house. He made a great many phone calls, but nobody came to that first meeting. So the first time he actually saw the Amway Sales and Marketing Plan was in his own home with just his wife and the **marker man.** Ashley describes that first meeting:

Rick came and showed the plan, with nobody there except [my wife] and me. I was kind of impressed by it but I was still rather skeptical at the same time. He said, 'don't make a decision now. See the plan two or three more times, and then decide what you want to do.' So he set up two more house meetings at my house. We did a little better each time as far as people who were attending. But still it was, you know, there weren't many people...[3]

Nobody was sponsored from those early meetings.

Family Reunion

In June, Rick started this spiel about Family Reunion at the last meeting he showed at my house. And when I found out how much it was, I said, 'no' I don't want to spend money on that. I hadn't even signed in as a distributor yet. [My wife] started getting on my case, started pressuring me that 'we gotta go, we gotta go. That's where people make decisions about the business' and all this stuff. It was a real battle.[4]

Until now, the real interest in the business came from Ashley's wife I asked him whether that ever changed, if there was a point when he became more interested for himself.

I guess it was Family Reunion. We ended up going to Boulder, CO. and I slowly began to get programmed, the way people do. I started to like Rick and Mary Jane more and more, trusted them more and more. They basically said, 'do what we do' and I started showing the plan. I think it was right after Family Reunion.[5]

During his four-year involvement, Ashley describes his life as:

Well, it was pretty much hell. It was pretty much hell from the beginning. In the first place, I didn't have the time to go out prospecting, phone calling showing the plan, following up. . . I just plain didn't have the time. I was working on two video documentaries, and working at the university, and being a farmer, doing nature photography, I was doing all kinds of stuff. I just plain didn't have the time to do it, and they said 'that's why you should do the business.'

Well, I started believing that because they said 'well, it'll free you up the time to do things that you want to do.' But it was real difficult. All the stress of not having the time, just the chaos of trying to work all this business activity in with everything else that I was doing caused a whole lot of stress. Constant fights between [my wife] and me, but the comment was, 'oh, just stick with it, all this means you're paying the price. It's the price you have to pay. All the miles you put on the car, all the stress, it means you're working the business the way you're supposed to.'[6]

Charles' Story

Charles, a computer professional, joined Bill Britt's Amway organization in November of 1991. He was sponsored by his stepson, who had joined a short time before. Charles' wife went to a meeting with her son, in an attempt to talk him out of it and ended up being interested herself.

Actually my wife wanted me to go to a Seminar & Rally with her. And of course this was during the playoff season for football, I was angry about that. A Diamond from Canada came there, and the guy made sense, or at least it sounded like it. And then I went ahead and got started.[7]

Charles' stepson is still actively involved in the Amway business. After eight years, he is still at the level of about 1500 PV.

Charles describes himself as being a core distributor during the five years he spent in the business. He went to all the functions he qualified to attend, was on standing order for tapes and books, and showed the plan. His life during that time was:

Hectic. It just seemed like every spare moment was involved in going to meetings, and the weekend meetings, and on weekends traveling to distance groups and trying to get things going there. Those kinds of things. We only had like one or two real vacations during that time period. I reckon the best way I can describe it is just hectic.[8]

Jason's Story

Jason Greenfield is a young, single professional in the computer industry. A co-worker, a young woman he became friends with and took to lunch occasionally, introduced him to the INA motivational organization, with Diamond Larry McCracken. His recruitment is quite typical. He describes the way his co-worker enticed him with the **curiosity approach**:

She would bring it into conversations. I'd ask her 'what do you want to do, what are your goals for the future, and what do you want to be doing' and things like that. And she'd basically respond, 'well I have this business with some of my friends,' and she was going to make a lot of money and be very successful. And from that she hoped to retire soon. She was talking maybe five to ten years, she didn't give any specific amount of time. And that sparked my interest. I said, 'well what are you talking about? Is this up and coming? Is this a small startup, something like that?' And she pretty much put it off. I'm an engineer so I'm obviously very curious, and she wouldn't give me any more information and that was that.

At some point maybe two or three weeks later, she finally e-mailed me over the company e-mail, and said, 'well we can meet either Monday or Tuesday'. Wasn't much choice, but I said 'sure.' I wanted to meet Monday and get it off my mind because it was still bothering me, I was curious. And finally Monday came around and I went to meet her, but it wasn't just her but it was her and her sponsor. The initial thoughts from me were that he was very pushy, very sure of himself, very confident, and it was pretty much this was the thing to do. I never really heard anything about Amway. The name was never mentioned.[9]

The focus of that initial meeting, according to Jason, was that with this as-yet-unnamed business, the consumer/distributor could save a lot of money by "buying wholesale from his own store." The name "Amway" was never mentioned. Jason agreed to go to another meeting in hopes that he would get more information. He describes the **love bombing** that he experienced at that meeting.

It was interesting. As soon as you walk in the door people are gathered around you, 'oh, who is this?' And everybody's interested to meet you and it's sort of this camaraderie thing, and everybody agrees with what you say, there's yes people everywhere talking about the same things.[10]

At this meeting, Jason finally found out that the business was Amway, and that he was one of a very few – perhaps the only – prospect there.

I didn't know what to think except to think that everybody was already in on this, everybody was pretty much a distributor there. And they were. There really weren't too many other prospects, there, nobody that I talked to at that point.

It was at that point that I really started to wonder what was going on. These people were sitting there talking about 'how can we reel these people in?' They're sitting there going, 'well, if this person's this personality type, here's how you can change your opinion, or change your facial expression, the way you talk to them, and try to get them to see your viewpoint, or at least to put their defenses down so that maybe they'll accept your tape or your CD or what you want to say and maybe invite them to something else.' They actually were giving instruction on how to modify your own body language depending on who you were talking to to make them trust you more.

And it was at that point that I met one of my sponsor's friends – many of her friends – but one lady that was in particular pretty pushy and went, 'oh, get in this business, this is the greatest business, don't really think about it, there's nothing to think about. If you think about it too long you're not going to want to do it, it's just numbers so get in the business and be done with it.' And I'm thinking, 'gosh, she's awfully pushy. What does she know that I don't know?'[11]

After this meeting, Jason decided to get the Business Kit. Most of his questions were still unanswered, and he believed that the only way he could really get the information he was looking for was to buy the kit. He was very focused on the pricing/money-saving aspect of the business, which had been heavily promoted to him at those early meetings.

So I jumped in and I got the kit, got the products, and started going through the bucketload of literature. And that's when I started having major problems with it considering that nobody told me about this Ten Customer Rule, or [the] 70% Rule, and then, pretty much nobody told me about any of the other rules that were throughout the book. Actually I thought it was quite complicated, this whole system of payments and things, and they make it sound like it's so easy and there's really nothing to it.[12]

Jason began studying the *Amway Business Compendium*, and was surprised by a lot of information there. He learned about the **Ten Customer Rule** and the **70% Rule** from the *Compendium*. The Ten Customer Rule (which has since been changed to the **50 PV Rule**) simply stated that a distributor had to sell product to ten customers to be eligible for a performance bonus. This rule was one of the reasons the FTC decided in 1979 that Amway was not an illegal pyramid scheme. It has never, to my knowledge, been enforced.[13] The 70% Rule states that 70% of the products you order must be sold at retail to consumers. The existence of this rule, which is also not enforced, contributed the the FTC ruling in 1979.

> *I looked at the pricing and I looked at these rules, and I said, well, it looks like until you get this huge customer base – or at least a decent one – I don't see how I'm going to be making money, because I'm not going to get paid. I mean, the Ten Customer Rule is right there. Besides that, I looked at the wholesale prices, I added up a couple of them, and I said, well, here's toilet paper, here's tissue, here's toothpaste and things. If you bought them in great bulk the prices possibly equaled something you could go to the store and get. Of course they weren't any great name brands. The prices don't even touch [come close to] if you buy bulk at Price Costco [a discount warehouse type of store]. So right away I had this big problem. I said, 'what is this business about if the prices aren't what you say they are.' These aren't wholesale prices, you can call them whatever you want but they aren't wholesale. And that was my biggest gripe. Why would you do this if the prices were bad?*
>
> *But a lot of people it just seems that once they get in that system where they have all these people that are attentive to them and at least want to seem like they're friends, they're happier.'[14]*

Roberta's Story

Roberta is a charming young woman from Italy. I'm including her story here because, even though she lives and had her Amway business in Europe, her experience shows clearly that the AMO experience is the same worldwide. Roberta agreed to see the plan because the person who contacted her was a very dear friend, and she was at a vulnerable time in her life.

> There are some times in our lives that everything seems to be perfect, everything goes as we believe it must go. And there are some others that it's not like this. We seem to need something else. The job doesn't fulfill us, lifestyles seems not good and the money isn't enough. I was living a moment like this when I met Amway. I was looking for that something else when I was contacted by a very close and dear person that told me she had an idea that would be the solution for my problems.

> Being curious I discovered that it had something with products and I didn't want to know more about that, but as the person who told me about was a very dear one, I decided to hear it just to please her. Then a very smiling man came to my home and in less than a couple of hours made me tell him all my problems and desires. And in a very clever way, as a way to realize my dreams, he showed me the [Amway Sales and Marketing] Plan, emphasizing how I'd realize all my wishes through that strange business.

> I began to believe that the only way to earn money and realize my dreams was that business. My very well trained sponsor told me that I really needed a meeting. That if I really wanted to reach my goals, I couldn't refuse it, because there was no one successful in the business that hadn't 'pass through' a meeting. And I began to follow his advice, and hear him more than my dear ones. I believed I was going to be successful in a couple of years, and then I'd be able to dedicate all my time to my dear ones.[15]

What is the thread that these widely different sponsoring experiences have in common? In one word, deception.

THREE: A Brief History of Amway Corporation

The Founders

Amway was started in 1959 by two lifelong friends, Rich DeVos and Jay Van Andel, in Grand Rapids, Michigan. The company started with a single product, an all-purpose organic cleaner which they called *Frisk*. DeVos and Van Andel had been business partners before in several other ventures. One of these was Nutrilite, a small California-based company selling food supplements. They had become Nutrilite distributors in 1949.

DeVos and Van Andel did well as distributors for a time, but then Nutrilite began to have problems. The company that ran the distributor operations and the company that produced the product experienced some friction, and DeVos and Van Andel decided to distance themselves from the fracas at Nutrilite. In 1959, with their former Nutrilite distributors, they began their new venture. In his book *The Possible Dream*, Charles Paul Conn quotes Jay Van Andel:

> In the direct-sales business, one must decide whether he wants an organization of highly specialized, professional salesmen, or a situation in which almost anyone can develop the business and make a profit. We opted for the latter approach. We wanted to provide an opportunity that

virtually any hard-working person could take advantage of.[1] (Conn, 22-3)

The distributor force grew, and the partners bought out the supplier and began manufacturing the product themselves, as well as adding other products to the line. They bought property in nearby Ada, Michigan and built homes for themselves. DeVos and Van Andel and their wives built the business, adding office help as needed. After a year, they bought an old gas station and installed their first office and print shop there. In 1972, with sales figures over $100 million, Amway bought the Nutrilite Corporation and brought it into the Amway fold.

The Corporation

The Amway business has expanded worldwide. Its first foreign market was Canada, which was eased into as distributors on the northern states bordering Ontario began sponsoring people across the border. Amway then gradually spread into Puerto Rico, brought there by distributors who had been sponsored in New York. In 1970, Australia opened to the Amway business, followed by England in 1972, Hong Kong in 1973, and Germany in 1975. Over the years, more countries were added. The People's Republic of China was opened for business in 1995. Today, Amway operates in 44 countries around the globe. In 1996, Amway opened in Greece, Costa Rica, and Colombia; in 1997 new countries included the Philippines and Romania, with India and Venezuela in 1998.

The product line has increased from the original organic cleaner to include services as well as products. Distributors routinely claim up to 10,000 products. But Amway itself admits to only about 450 products, with other products available by catalog in limited markets.

During the 1990s, the original co-founders turned over the day-to-day running of the company to their sons. Dick DeVos replaced his father as President of Amway Corporation, and Steve Van Andel took over as Chairman of the Board. The Amway Policy Board – comprising **Founding Family** members only – was formed, and includes Rich DeVos and Jay Van Andel, along with children Dick, Doug and Dan DeVos, Cheri DeVos Vander Weide, Steve, Dave and Nan Van Andel and Barb Van Andel Gaby.

Amway has been called the "granddaddy" of **multilevel marketing (MLM)**. Products are distributed exclusively through a distributor network – with the exception of the People's Republic of China.[2] When DeVos and Van Andel started Amway, they had five "front line" distributors. From these five, a network of three million distributors worldwide has sprung. A distributor can earn money in one of two ways: by selling product, or by collecting bonuses based on sponsoring new distributors and on the total volume of his business combined with his distributors' businesses.

Amway has frequently been accused of being an illegal pyramid scheme. Several court decisions have said it is not. A landmark Federal Trade Commission (FTC) ruling in 1979 ordered Amway to cease its price-fixing activities and stop misrepresenting income potential to new recruits. At the same time, the FTC determined that Amway was not a pyramid scheme because it

- had no headhunting fee
- made product sales a precondition for receiving the performance bonus
- bought back unsold inventory and
- required a substantial amount of product to be bought by customers at retail.

However, as we will demonstrate later, the characteristics of the Amway business that made it "not an illegal pyramid scheme" in 1979 have changed. Virtually no product is sold at retail today in North America – actual retail sales comprise only about 18% of all Amway sales. The other 82% is personal consumption by distributors.

The *Amway Business Review*, or *SA4400*, is a document which Amway distributors are required by the FTC to give to prospective recruits when they introduce them to the business, or show the plan. The SA4400 is supposed to fairly and accurately represent the income potential of the Amway business. According to the *SA4400*, dated January, 1997 and revised January, 1998, "**The Average Monthly Gross Income for 'Active' Distributors Was $88.**"[3] This, of course, is before expenses.

The Sales and Marketing Plan

Let's define a few terms, and then briefly summarize the Amway Sales and Marketing Plan.

1. **Basic Discount** is the difference between the amount a distributor pays for a product and the amount he is able to sell it for. This is often called **Immediate Profit**.

2. **Point Value (PV)** "is a unit amount assigned to each product; it determines your Performance Bonus bracket."[4] (SA4400) This is an arbitrary number assigned by Amway to each product or service. Your PV determines your monthly bonus percentage.

3. **Business Volume (BV)** "is a dollar figure for each product. It is used for the calculation of monthly and annual bonuses."[5] (SA4400) This is another number assigned by Amway Corp. to each piece of merchandise or service. The BV is somewhat related to the actual cost of the item. Monthly bonuses are calculated on BV. When showing the Plan, distributors usually claim a 1:2 ratio of PV to BV, although this is not always the case.

4. **Performance Bonus** is a bonus based on a percentage of your PV and paid on the same percentage of the BV; the monthly bonus you receive for the volume of goods and services which passes through your sales organization.

5. **Group Volume.** The sum of all goods and services you purchase from Amway, plus the sum of all the goods and services purchased by the distributors you've sponsored, the distributors they've sponsored, etc.

6. **Active Distributor,** according to an independent survey conducted from April 1994-March 1995, is a distributor who "attempted to make a retail sale, or presented the Sales and Marketing Plan, or received bonus money, or attended a company or distributor meeting in the month surveyed. ... Approximately 41% of all distributors were found to be 'active'."[6] (SA4400)

7. **Downline** includes the distributors you sponsor, those they sponsor, and so on *ad infinitum.*

8.   Profit, as used in the Plan, does not really mean profit. It simply indicates the difference between the bonus Amway pays you and what you pay out in turn to your distributors. It does *not* reflect your true profit.

The Amway Sales and Marketing Plan, Summarized

First, let us preface our explanation of Amway's Sales and Marketing Plan by saying that the plan is extremely complicated. I have heard a number of successful distributors make statements in public to the effect that, "I don't know how Amway calculates the Emerald (or Diamond, or Direct Distributor) bonus, I just know that I get my checks on time." Any discussion of the **Plan** is inherently – and I believe intentionally – confusing.

We will use the same assumptions that the Sales and Marketing Plan makes. The first of these is that each distributor will purchase at least 100 PV in products and services each month, for personal consumption and/or to resell at retail. (In real dollar terms, 100 PV equals about $226.00.)

Amway Bonus Schedule	
Total Monthly Point Value	Perfornace Bonus (% of BV)
100	3
300	6
600	9
1000	12
1500	15
2500	18
4000	21
6000	23
7500	25
10000	Additional 1%
12500	Additional 2%
15000	Additional 3%

Table 1

<u>Step One: Sell Something.</u> The first way to make money in Amway is to sell something. Amway is not allowed to dictate retail prices, but there is a difference of anywhere from 10% to 50% between what the distributor pays for the product (**distributor cost**, or **wholesale**), and what he sells it for (**suggested retail**). This difference is called the **Basic Discount, Immediate Profit** or **markup**. The Plan presumes an "average" markup of 30%. Let's say you end the month with 100 PV/200 BV. Let's also say that you sell at retail every product you purchased from your upline that month. If you spend $200.00 (your distributor cost) for products, and sell them for $260.00, you've just made $60.00. This is your Immediate Profit. The Sales and Marketing Plan you show your prospects presupposes this Immediate Profit each and every month.

Step Two: Earn a Performance Bonus. The second way to make money in Amway is through the Performance Bonus. This bonus is paid according to a performance scale. The scale, arbitrarily assigned by Amway Corp., ranges from 100 PV to 15,000 PV (see Table 1). At 100 PV, the Performance Bonus is 3%, which equals $6.00 (if the 1:2 ratio of PV:BV is accurate). Thus, in your hypothetical first month, you would earn a whopping $66.00 – before expenses – when you combine your Immediate Profit and your Performance Bonus.

Step Three: Sponsor People. The third way to make money in Amway is to sponsor some people who sell something. "Distributors who sponsor others generally have higher average volume than those who don't sponsor."[7] (SA4400) (Well, of course!) Amway's Sales and Marketing Plan assumes that you'll sponsor six distributors who each generate 100 PV/200 BV. Some of the distributor organizations show their own variation on this scenario, drawing out marketing plans that show "you" sponsoring nine, who in turn sponsor four (or six), who sponsor two (or three). Amway instructs its distributors to caution prospects at the beginning of each meeting that "The examples I will use are simply to show you how the Plan works. They are not intended to project or promise any actual earnings."[8] (Amway, "Sponsoring")

(The rest of this chapter is very number-intensive. If you're not interested in the minutiae of Amway's Sales and Marketing Plan, you may want to jump ahead.)

Let's follow Amway's example from the *SA4400* for your hypothetical first six months in business. Remember, these are *Amway's* numbers and examples.

Month One: You earn $66.00 by doing Step One: you sell 100 PV/200 BV at retail. This generates $60.00 Immediate Profit, and you make the Step Two Performance Bonus of $6.00

Month Two: You earn $150.00. You do Step One (same as *Month One* above) and Step Two. You also do Step Three: You sponsor six distributors who each do Step One (purchase 100 PV/200 BV.) Your total group volume (your personal volume plus the volume of each distributor in your group, or downline) will be 700 PV/1400 BV. According to Amway's bonus schedule, you qualify for a 9% bonus, or $126.00. Since each of your distributors did Steps One and Two, each is entitled to a Performance Bonus – 3% of 200 BV, or $6.00. After you've paid each distributor his Performance Bonus (a total of $36.00), you're left with

$90.00. You also have the $60.00 immediate profit from your sales, for a gross income that month of $150.00.

Month Three: The following month, each of your six personally sponsored distributors does Steps One, Two and Three: each sponsors four, and everybody still generates 100 PV. There are now five distributors in each of your groups (the person you sponsored, plus the four that he sponsored). The PV for each of your personally sponsored groups is 500, and your total group volume is 3100 PV/6200 BV (six groups at 500 PV plus your personal 100 PV). At 3100 PV you qualify for an 18% Performance Bonus, or $1,116.00 (6200 BV times eighteen percent). Since each of your personally sponsored distributors had a group volume of 500 PV/1000 BV, they are entitled to a 6% bonus, or $60.00 apiece. After you pay out the $360.00, you're left with $756 plus your $60.00 immediate profit for a gross income of $816.00.

		Profit and Bonuses According to Amway's SA4400		
Month	**Immediate Profit**	**Performance Bonus**	**Pay to Downline**	**Total Gross Income**
Month One	$60.00	$6.00	$0.00	$66.00
Month Two	60.00	126.00	36.00	150.00
Month Three	60.00	1116.00	360.00	816.00
Month Four	60.00	3950.00	1872.00	2138.00
Month Five	60.00	3950.00	1872.00	2138.00
Month Six	60.00	3950.00	1872.00	2138.00

Table 2

Month Four: Each of the four distributors sponsored by your personal people sponsors just two new distributors. Again assuming everyone generates 100 PV/200 BV, your entire group volume would be 7900 PV. This places you in the 25% Performance Bonus bracket. Twenty-five percent of your BV of 15,800 is $3,950. Each of your personal groups at this point has a PV of 1300, so you pay each of them $312.00 (2600 BV times twelve percent). After paying out the $1872.00 total ($312 times six personal groups), you're left with $2,078.00 plus your $60.00 immediate profit, for an income of $2,138.00 that month, before expenses.

According to a box inset on the SA4400, "One out of every 45 'active' distributors actually achieved the hypothetical monthly BV performance illustrated above in at least one month during the 12-month survey period."[9] (SA4400) Since only 41% of all distributors are active, this means that only 0.0091, or less than 1% of all distributors, achieve the 7500 PV level for even one month out of the year.

Months Five and Six: You maintain your 7500 PV level and become a **Gold Producer.**

Upon reaching and maintaining the 25% Performance Bonus bracket for six months out of the fiscal year, with at least three of those months being consecutive, and with some restrictions as to how your group is structured, you achieve **Direct Distributor** status. "The survey and company records show that approximately... 2% of all 'active' distributors met Direct Distributor qualification requirements during the survey period."[10] (SA4400) Translated, this means that fewer than 1% of all distributors qualify as Direct Distributors.

Amway claimed 700,000 distributors in North America for the fiscal year September 1, 1996 - August 31, 1997. According to their own figures, then, only 287,000 of those are active. This would translate into 5,740 **qualified** Direct Distributors.

After qualifying as a DD, you are eligible for a number of additional bonuses. There is a **Leadership Bonus**, as well as bonuses named for various gemstones: **Sapphire** (formerly **Pearl**), **Emerald, Diamond** and

An Emerald Direct Distributor is a Direct Distributor who sponsors three qualified Direct Distributor legs. If there are 5,740 qualifed Direct Distributors in North America, this would create a maximum of 1435 Emerald Directs (5,740 divided by four: the Emerald Direct and three Direct Distributor legs). A Diamond Direct Distributor sponsors six qualified Direct Distributor legs. Therefore, North America would have no more than 820 Diamonds. This is only 0.117% of all distributors. (There are actually fewer than 800 distributors who have qualified for Diamond even once in Amway's 40-year history – but who may not be qualified now.)

Distributor Information From Amway's SA4400			
	Total North American Distributors*	Percentage of Total Distributors	Ratio
All Distributors	700,000	41	1/45
Distributors who reach 7500 PV in any single month (est.)	6,378	0.91	1/110
Qualified Direct Distributors (est.)	5,740	0.82	1/122
Qualified Emerald Diriect Distributors (est.)	1,435	0.205	1/3484
Qualified Diamond Direct Distributors (est.)	820	0.117	1/6,098
Table 3			

Crown. Qualifications for these bonuses are not based on personal group volume – that would be too simple! Instead, you qualify by having groups within your **downline** who are at the Direct Distributor level.

The process of introducing a new prospect to the business is called **Showing the Plan (STP)** or **Drawing Circles**. There are three settings for showing the plan: one-on-one in the prospect's home or over a cup of coffee in a restaurant, at a **house meeting**, where the prospect invites as many friends and relatives as he can to come and see it together, or you can take your prospects to see the plan at an **Introductory Seminar**. The majority of new recruits are introduced to the business at a one-on-one. The person showing the plan at a one-on-one or a house meeting will usually be the new distributor's **sponsor** or someone else in the **immediate upline**. (The "immediate upline" is a distributor in the direct line of sponsorship above. In other words, if I am the new distributor, and you are my sponsor, and Fred sponsors you, then both you and Fred are part of my immediate upline. Fred's sponsor George might also be considered immediate upline if he works closely in this leg.)

Typically, a new distributor will have two or three house meetings with help from his upline. From those meetings, the upline will choose the **sharpest** prospect to work with, leaving the new distributor to follow up with the castoffs.

In most Amway distributor organizations in North America, products are moved through a **line of sponsorship**. This means, as a new distributor, you place your order with your sponsor for whatever products and services you want to purchase yourself, as well as any sales you've made. Your sponsor then places a combined order with his sponsor, who places a combined order with his sponsor, up to the nearest Direct Distributor who orders directly from Amway Corporation. After you sponsor someone, your new **downline** distributor will place his order with you, you place a combined order with your sponsor, and so on up the line of sponsorship.

Performance Bonuses are also paid through the line of sponsorship. Amway pays the Direct Distributor, who then pays each of his personally sponsored distributors, who each pay their personally sponsored distributors, and so on down the line.

This system is gradually changing. Amway's distributors in all international markets order from the Amway affiliate in their country, and receive bonus payments directly; gradually the North American market is conforming to that pattern. Several of the largest Diamond organizations already use this **direct fulfillment** system, where each distributor deals directly with Amway; other organizations will be brought into the direct fulfillment fold by September 1, 1999.

FOUR: What are Tools?

tool, n. 1. An implement, esp. one held in the hand, for performing or facilitating mechanical operations, as a hammer, saw, file, etc. 2. Any instrument of manual operation. 3. The cutting or machining part of a lathe, planer, drill, or similar machine. 4. The machine itself; a machine tool. 5. Anything used as a tool. 6. A person manipulated by another for his own ends; cat's-paw.[1] (Random House *Dictionary*, 1967, 1493)

Depending upon one's line of work, a tool could be a pen, a computer, a screwdriver, a paintbrush, a musical instrument, or any number of "implements." In the Amway business, tools comprise five basic categories: books, tapes, functions, sales aids, and the newest, high-tech communications media. Tools are also referred to as **Business Support Materials,** or **BSMs.** When distributors started creating and distributing their own tools, the Amway business changed dramatically from what DeVos and Van Andel had created.

Books

Amway distributors are fond of quoting motivational speaker and author Charlie "Tremendous" Jones: "Where you will be in five years depends on the books you read and the people you associate with." Distributors are strongly encouraged to read, but not just any reading will do. Newspapers and news magazines are out – they're **negative**, and negative thinking must be banished if we're to succeed. Novels are out – they don't teach success principles. A distributor should only read books which will contribute to his success. This includes anything written by anyone named Yager, books by motivational authors like Zig Ziglar, Norman Vincent Peale or Dennis Waitley, books about business which present the Amway business in a positive light, and **personal growth** books. Books, according to your sponsor, will help you grow as a person, and that will help your business grow.

Tapes

Audio tapes (and more recently, audio Compact Discs, which we will include in the tape category) provide "information and motivation." You can listen to tapes while driving in your car, shaving, applying makeup, dressing, doing housework, and especially you can listen to tapes while on your way to draw circles. Tapes get you pumped up and excited about the business.

There are **teaching** tapes and **rally** tapes. Teaching tapes discuss a specific topic: how to prospect, how to do a home meeting, how to follow up with a prospect, and a few of them even mention products! Rally tapes are personal stories. The distributor or distributor couple talk about their life before the business, and some of their experiences with the business.

Tapes can also be used as prospecting tools. There are many **generic** tapes available, tapes that don't mention Amway, which are handed out to pique the curiosity of your prospect and pave the way for showing the plan. "Followup" tapes are designed for your prospect after he's seen the plan, to minimize the questions he will have for you.

Music tapes are also available. These are heavily promoted at **functions**. Music tapes, according to the leadership, will help you when your morale is low. When you pop that tape into your player on your way home after a **no-show**, you'll mentally be right back in the coliseum with 40,000 excited distributors around you, and you'll be able to relive the excitement you felt at the function. It will help you over your hump. Music is so important!

Functions

Functions is the catch-all term used to describe a wide variety of meeting types, including **Introductory Seminars, Seminars & Rallies, Regional Rallies,** and **major functions** – huge gatherings of distributors from a wide geographic area having catchy names like *Family Reunion, Dream Weekend,* or *Free Enterprise Day.* There are also special Leadership Meetings, which distributors must qualify to attend.

Sales Aids

Sales aids include product catalogs, order forms, price lists, pamphlets, handouts, informational brochures, and in a few cases audio or video tapes which describe or demonstrate a specific product.

Communications Media

Although this category is not yet part of the litany of "books, tools and functions" taught to distributors, it has become a strong and compelling tool. The broad heading of "communications media," includes the Amvox Voice Messaging System (VoiceTel in Canada), and proprietary satellite television channels available through cable providers. (We also anticipate either Amway or some of the major distributor leaders to offer proprietary on-line computer services in the near future.) Each of these has the added advantage to the AMO leaders of generating ongoing, residual revenue on a monthly basis.

Amvox is the voice messaging system sold by Amway Corp. In addition to basic "answering machine" services, the Amvox system has networking capabilities. This means that "A" can send a message to "B," who can then pass it along to "C," "D," and "E." Each of them in turn might send it to eight or ten more distributors who could forward it to another twenty or thirty, and so on. This way, instead of messaging your downline distributor to say that your upline told you something, you pass along the upline's actual message, in his or her own words, keeping the **duplication** pure. Interestingly, the use of this system has become a key point in several of the recent lawsuits against Amway.

Costs of this system are also extremely high. The "Basic Answer" Amvox, which does not offer networking features and works like an answering machine, costs $11.85 per month, or $9.50 at distributor cost. I have the same service through my local telephone company for $4.95. VoiceTel, the company which provides the service which Amway resells, offers the same services directly. Any individual, small business, or organization can set up a networked voice messaging system, and for less money. What Amway sells as the Premier service for $27.95 ($22.35 distributor cost) is available directly for $19.95. Because Amvox is sold by Amway, it carries PV and BV, and provides **residual income** for distributors.

The "Achievers Channel" is a proprietary satellite channel created for InterNET Services Corp., the tool arm of the empire of distributors Dexter and Birdie Yager. This channel promises to deliver content that will help distributors in their line of sponsorship to sponsor and train new recruits, and to promote the lifestyles of the high achievers. Information publicizing the channel in October, 1997, promised that it will deliver 45 hours of programming each month, including **Credibility Segments**, to be used as "closers" after showing the plan; **Diamond Showcases**, which would air immediately following the credibility segment; Amway product infomercials, and BSM infomercials. The cost to distributors? Only $39.95 per month!

We speculate that some sort of on-line computer service will be offered to Amway distributors.* Several years ago, Amway Corp. struck a deal with CompuServe to provide proprietary content on the CompuServe system. This was known as the Amway Business Network, or ABN. Distributors who wanted access to ABN could enroll with Compuserve, and access ABN for an additional fee each month. ABN has since moved to the World Wide Web, and the proprietary content removed from the CompuServe network. However, we believe that Amway will be forced to offer a proprietary network of some sort, for two important reasons: first, to capture the residual moneys that distributors are now paying to other internet service providers; and second, to offer its own proprietary content and thus keep distributors off certain World Wide Web sites. Why? Because the internet has become a powerful tool which allows those who have been financially or emotionally harmed by

---

* As we go to press, the internet and Amvox are buzzing with news of an approaching internet-based business which will be called *QUIXTAR*, **not** "Amway," but which will be owned by the DeVos and Van Andel families and will sell Amway products. While no details of this business have been

their Amway experience to disseminate information that Amway and the distributor leaders don't want publicized.

Who Provides the Tools?

Some of the tools, primarily sales aids, are produced by Amway Corp. These are sold to distributors and carry no **PV**, although most do carry **BV**. Therefore, the purchase of catalogs or other sales aids will not help a distributor qualify for a bonus level, but his bonus payment will reflect those purchases. Amway also offers a handful of audiotapes and videos. The vast majority of tools, however, do not come from Amway.

In the September, 1997 SA-13 Wholesale Price List, the most recent available as of this writing, Amway offered videos dealing with commercial laundry products, home care product demonstrations, home laundry care, the Amway-branded vacuum cleaner, cookware, nutrition products, personal care and cosmetics, Amvox and Franklin Quest®, the brand of time planner marketed by Amway. Non-product videos numbered only thirteen. Several of these are sponsoring aids, four show lifestyles of high achievers, and one is founder Rich DeVos' video talk about his book *Compassionate Capitalism*. Price for the videos is $15.00 apiece, with 15.00 BV.

Audio tapes offered by Amway are few in number as well: eight product-related audio tapes, at $4.00 each with 4.00 BV; and 17 that are not product-oriented, 14 of which feature either Rich DeVos or Jay Van Andel, company co-founders.

---

finalized, distributor websites trolling for prospects are going online at a rapid rate. Ken McDonald, Vice President of Amway North America (ANA), sent out an Amvox message to Emeralds and above where he discussed the "family friendly" internet service that will be available from Amway. This service, according to McDonald, would "offer a family-friendly Internet service provider that will filter out all those 'bad-guy' web sites you want to keep from invading your family's PC." [Amvox message from Ken McDonald, January 21, 1999.] Will distributors have a choice about which sites are filtered, or is this an attempt by Amway to keep distributors from accessing the sites which are critical of Amway or the AMOs?

All other Amway-produced support materials listed fall into the category of sales aids: brochures, customer handouts, samples, dispensers, demonstrators, or replacement parts.

So who does provide the tools of the system? Enter the Yagers.

Dexter and Birdie Yager are Crown Ambassador Direct Distributors, meaning that they personally sponsor at least 20 Direct Distributor organizations. They became Amway distributors in 1964. At the time, they lived in Rome, NY with four small children. Yager was a salesman for the West End Brewery, making $95.00 per week setting up Utica Club beer displays in grocery stores. The Yagers became Direct Distributors very quickly, but three years later their business had slipped so much that Yager was applying for jobs.

Then somebody loaned him a vinyl record of the famous Earl Nightingale motivational speech, *The Strangest Secret*. Yager turned his Amway business around. Dexter Yager had discovered the power of motivational tools, and he began selling them to his group during the 1970s.

While there are non-Yager Amway organizations which have similar motivational tool systems, we believe Yager's to have been the first, and to have established the pattern for the others.

Doug Wead is a minister and an Amway Diamond, although he is no longer recognized by the Yager organization (see sidebar). According to Wead, in taped speeches made during the 1980's, Dexter originally gave away motivational tapes to

The Amway Motivational Organizations like Yager's are adept at rewriting history. Distributors who meet with their disapproval for any reason simply disappear from the acknowledged history of the organization. Wead is no longer invited to speak, and his tapes are not offered for sale. This revision of history occurs routinely whenever there is a Diamond divorce. "Doug and Gloria Wead" disappear from view: Doug later re-surfaces as a motivational speaker, not as an Amway Diamond, and is married to Miriam. "Kenny and Donna Stewart" become "Kenny Stewart," and the organization pretends that Donna never existed. My diamond told me to get rid of any audio tapes that feature her, because she's no longer "plugged in." "Carlos and Carmen Marin" metamorphoses into Carlos and a new wife. "Bill and Hona Childers" is now "Bill and Suzee Childers." Bev and Jim Mainor disappear: Bev resurfaces as Bev Johnson, wife of Diamond Leif Johnson. Today, it's "Leif and Bonnie Johnson," and "Beverly Sallee" is a single Diamond. New distributors are given the impression that Kenny Stewart and the others built their businesses singlehandedly. After all, we don't want to acknowledge that the Diamonds get divorces just like anyone else – that would be negative!

his group, because he recognized that their businesses grew faster if distributors had these materials. After a time, he started charging for the tapes that he made available. Dexter claimed that distributors would listen to the tapes more and absorb the teaching better if they had to pay something for them, Wead explained.

From those humble beginnings, the Yagers have created a motivational empire, run by his company, InterNET Services Corp. Tools, or the system in Yager/InterNET parlance, includes motivational/educational tapes, books, videos, CDs, pamphlets, brochures, handouts, and most recently, a proprietary satellite television network available through a cable provider. Tools also includes a system of **functions**. These will be discussed later.

Standing Order Tape (SOT) and **Book of the Month (BOM)** are the backbone of the Yager tool business. There is a regular SOT, and also a **PaceSetter** or **QuickSilver** SOT. The latter, of course, is for the **real winners**, those distributors who are really **putting it together.** Some organizations have recently added a **Video of the Month (VOM)** as well. Once a distributor signs up for any of these standing orders, he is obligated to take each weekly tape, monthly book and video, at the prevailing price. He can request to be taken off standing order, but the pressure from his upline to continue receiving it is very strong, as will be demonstrated.

Many other tapes are available. Typically, speakers from Seminars, Rallies, and major functions are recorded, and those tapes made available later as either SOT or under another numbering system. The SOT tapes which are very popular are usually re-numbered and released later as well. Tape packs which combine major speakers from the larger functions are sold. Oftentimes, a distributor will buy one of these tape packs, only to find that he receives duplicate tapes, spread out over a period of weeks, through the SOT program.

There are also Inspirational or Christian tapes available through a separate SOT program. So a distributor who is heavily involved in the system can easily spend $18.00, plus tax and handling, each and every week for tapes that he doesn't choose. And of course, the SOTs, being "special orders" are non-returnable and non-refundable in spite of Amway's insistence that the producers of BSMs offer them with the same guarantee of returnability that Amway offers on its products and tools.

There are music tapes and CDs. There are videos which feature everything from a high-ranking Diamond showing the marketing plan to lifestyles videos showing all the houses, cars, boats, airplanes, jewelry, furs, and other toys that the Diamonds have. There is a limited selection of computer software.

There are generic tapes and videos, which don't mention Amway or selling. These insidious tools are designed to be used in prospecting new recruits. There are generic brochures and pamphlets to accompany those prospecting tapes.

The tool list also includes books: books authored by Dexter or Birdie Yager, motivational books by people like Zig Ziglar, books about business, about relationships, about marriage, about religion, and about politics. The BOM might be a little $3.00 pamphlet-type book, or it might be a $20.00 hardcover. Once a distributor has signed up for BOM, he takes what's sent, and pays for it.

Until recently, InterNET's list of tapes and books included almost nothing about selling Amway products. In mid-1997, in an unusual effort to showcase sales and products, there was a sudden flurry of releases of tapes, brochures, and forms dealing with the new "automatic replenishment" or *Home Shopping Delivered/HSD* system. (This "new" system allows distributors to set themselves and customers up on an automatic ordering system, with purchases charged to a credit card.)

According to an article in the Charlotte, NC *Observer,* March 19, 1995:

The Pentagon of Yager's Amway army is a nondescript office-warehouse on Steele Creek Road in southwest Charlotte. InterNET Services Corp. serves as headquarters and supply depot. It distributes millions of books, tapes and videos that are the motivational fuel for Yager troops in their fight against slammed doors and 'negative people'. ... InterNET Services [is] now a $35 million a year business.[2]

InterNET Services Corp. provides motivational tools to Yager Amway organizations in a number of different countries, including the United States, Canada, Mexico, Costa Rica, El Salvador, Honduras, Guatemala, Colombia, Great Britain, France, Germany, Italy, Spain, Hungary, Poland, Czech Republic, Slovakia, Slovenia, Romania, Switzerland, Greece, Belgium, Netherlands, Portugal, Philippines, Australia, New Zealand, India, Venezuela, South Africa and China[3] as of this writing. However, we will be discussing the tool business primarily as it exists in North America: the United States and Canada.

FIVE: Money and the Tools

For years as a distributor, I was assured that the motivational tools existed only to help distributors, that they were fairly priced, and nobody made a profit on tools. This is simply not true.

Can You Get Your Money Back?

One of Amway's strong selling points is their 100% guarantee. If a customer is dissatisfied with a product for any reason at all, Amway will take it back, and will even pay the return shipping. Returning motivational tools, however, is nearly impossible. The return is totally dependent on the good will of the upline, up to and including the upline Diamond. As one disgruntled former distributor explained in an e-mail message:

I was an active distributor for more than one year and during that time I purchased a lot of tapes, books, etc. at the urging of my upline and the 'system'.

While I was active, one of my distributors left the business and wanted a refund on her Business Support Materials (tapes, books, tool kit). I asked my upline direct if I could do this and he said yes. We refunded her 97% – he said 3% was a re-stocking fee. That was fair. All were pleased.

When I left the business, my upline direct was not fair. He told me that he refunded that money to my downline because he 'felt sorry for me' and 'didn't want my friend to be upset with me.' He said that he would have to check with his upline to see if he could give me a refund. That was a month ago. I am going to follow up with him tonight. I know he is going to give me a hard time.

All I'm asking for is the same treatment as my downline received. Why does one business get 97% back from a tool refund while the other business (me) will maybe get a 25% refund? Sounds like the rules are made up as they go along...very unethical.[1]

Another distributor has shared the same, in a series of letters. This man was a distributor for four years and describes himself as a **believer** in the Amway business and the motivational system. He explains,

But in the end we were the losers. We lost financially, time and almost a marriage.

Over the past nine months I have tried to recoup some of the tool money. I followed [InterNET Service Corp.'s] advice. One month at least later I get a call [from my upline] saying they are unable to return the tools because it would be too disruptive and cause too much of a problem. They said they would resell them though. I did not care what happened to them as long as I was reimbursed. After six months I had $68.00 out of $600.00. Can you believe it?

The reason we got out was because of the way the tool system worked. When I started questioning and trying to get some refunds, we were turned away. Black balled. No one will speak to us, not even people we were really close to. My upline diamond was Greg Howard then Everett Davis [upline Emerald], then Dick Kangas [Direct Distributor]. I know there are others in there but these are the key players.

Since our last conversation I have gotten the ear of a Diamond and the Amway Corp. Once I did that my Direct has tried to buy my silence for $100 out of $600. . . He still does not get it. He denies any knowledge of how to return any tools to InterNET. Oh yeah – no one in his upline which takes us up to Tim Bryan [a Diamond personally sponsored by Dexter Yager] knows how to return tools either. I just can not believe it they say they are your friend but as soon as you stop forget it.[2]

Why should it be so difficult to get refunds on tools?

In 1995, Tom Eggleston, then chief operating officer of Amway Corp., insisted that the Yagers' motivational sideline posed no problems for the corporation.

'We are satisfied that the retail selling price is competitive with similar training materials in the marketplace and delivers good value for distributors,' he said. Eggleston said the corporation reviews many InterNET training materials and cassette tapes 'to assure that they fairly and accurately depict the earnings potential and other aspects of the business.' He said Amway has emphasized that purchase of such materials is voluntary."[3] (*Observer*, 19 Mar 1995)

Many distributors and former distributors disagree. In fact, there would seem to be disagreement at the highest corporate levels about the burgeoning motivational tools business. Cofounder Rich DeVos released a message to Direct Distributors in 1982 that clearly shows his objections. DeVos announced first that Amway was putting BV– but not PV – on the handful of motivational tapes in the Amway catalog, tapes that at that time sold for $2.50 in the US and $2.95 in Canada. This way, distributors could increase their Performance Bonus through tape sales in their groups. In his *Directly Speaking* tape, reproduced for court pleadings in the 1984 *Cairns vs. Amway* case, and a matter of public record, DeVos discusses what the tape business should not be:

> *Now, the tape business, if it is not used as a support for the Amway business, will oftentimes be an illegal business – in fact, it could be called a pyramid – because, d — does not get sold to the consumer. Which means that all the tape business does is take money out of the organization, and because the final person can't retail it, it never brings money into the organization. Now, I'm not arguing about the value of it – we accept the fact that motivation is vital to this business. Good, honest motivation is important to the business.* **But, it must be motivation that builds the business – not become a business in itself.** (Emphasis mine.)
>
> *You [speaking to the Directs] present wonderful numbers on the blackboard about all the money they [distributors] can make. Maybe you ought to tell them about all you're going to take from them [with your tools businesses] before they make any. Maybe that would be the rest of the story.*
>
> *And some of you have made it a business unto itself. And you're making a lot of money on it ...*[4] (*Cairns v. Amway*)

Therein lies the crux of the motivational tools business, which has led to many abuses. The tool business has generated huge incomes for a few people. For the sake of clarity, from this point forward any references to Amway or the Amway business will refer to Amway Corporation. The distributor lines of sponsorship which participate in these systems of books, tapes and functions, will be referred to as **Amway Motivational Organizations (AMOs)**.

The major North American AMOs are the Yager/InterNET system, Britt Worldwide, World Wide Dream Builders (WWDB), International Networking Associates (INA), International Leadership Development, Inc. (ILD), and Network 21. Bill and Peggy Britt (Britt Worldwide) are actually part of Dexter and Birdie Yager's organization; however, the Britts separated their AMO from Yager's in the early 1980's after Yager began manufacturing his own tapes. (Britt's business had previously handled tape duplication for both organizations.) WWDB is headed by Ron Puryear, whose upline is Bill and Peggy Britt. INA, headed by Jack Daughery, split from WWDB. In South America and Europe, another major AMO is ProNet, headed by Crown Direct Distributors Tim and Connie Foley. The Foleys are also downline from Yager in North America, but have created their own AMO overseas. Hal and Susan Gooch have recently withdrawn their large organization, which includes Crowns Kenny Stewart and Tim and Connie Foley, from under the Yager/InterNET umbrella.

The AMOs are all intertwined and inter-related, making it difficult to see how they fit together. It may be easier to visualize them in terms of a very large, multi-generational family. Since the Yager/InterNET system is the one the others sprang from, this is the AMO system we will focus on.

> Diana Lackey, a former InterNET [Services Corp.] employee... said Internet paid ICCA[5] 55 cents to duplicate each tape. The tapes were sold to 'Diamonds' for varying prices – usually $1 to $2 apiece, she said. But by the time they got to the newest recruits, the price had jumped to $5. More than 200 new InterNET tapes were released yearly and millions of tapes changed hands, she said.[6] (*Observer*, 20 March, 1995)

A commercial price list recently obtained from ICCA shows bulk tape duplication prices at 60 cents apiece. This is the price ICCA would charge a non-Amway business, and obviously includes ICCA's profit.

Different Diamond organizations charge different amounts, but in many organizations a single tape costs $6.00 in the United States, and one organization shows a price of $9.50 on tapes. When I was a new distributor, I attempted to order several of the motivational tapes produced by Amway Corp. (At that time, Yager was charging $3.00 for each tape, fifty cents more than Amway was charging.) My sponsor told me that those tapes were "not available" in our particular organization; this is a common practice throughout the Yager system. In the distributor organizations where only the Direct Distributor can place orders directly with Amway, the Direct simply does not order Amway Corp.'s motivational tools. This forces the distributor to get tapes from the upline system rather than from Amway, at a higher cost to the distributor, and a much higher profit to the upline.

Why Do Distributors Need Tools?

When a distributor asks his upline why he needs tools, he hears predictable responses. "Well, if you were a carpenter, you wouldn't think of going to work without your hammer, saw, screwdriver, etc. The tapes and books are your tools for building a successful Amway business." "Tools are optional, but so is success." "Every trade has its own tools." "If you want to become successful, you have to learn how successful people think. The tapes and books will help you do that." "Tools will help you grow as a person." "The tools will increase your sponsoring rate."

Tapes are important for information and motivation, you are told. Tapes will inspire you. Tapes will help you "overcome the negative," tapes will lift you out of your "stinkin' thinkin' J-O-B mentality." Tapes will help you sponsor new people. Never was I told, nor have I ever heard of another distributor who was told, "tapes will help you sell products."

Books serve a different purpose, the upline will explain. Books will educate you and help you change your thinking. Listening to a tape will motivate you; reading a book will inspire you. Reading is important because studies prove that you retain more of what you *see* than what you only *hear*.

The December, 1997 list of new tapes, books and videos available from InterNET Services Corp. for North America breaks tools down into categories: *Advertising Packs*, (one), actually not product advertising at all, but generic tapes which do not mention Amway, Products or Selling and which tout the advantages of becoming a distributor; *Merchandising/ Self-Use* (three); *Rally/Story*, (two); *Seminar/Teaching* (ten); *Commitment/Leadership: Family* (one); *Attitude, Commitment* (one); *Attitude/Self-Image/ Success* (one); *Follow Through* (one); *Inspirational* (one); *Showing the Plan* (two); *Singles* (one) and a category called *Next Generation* (two).

From analyzing distribution models in many industries I can tell you that the practice of profiting from selling "training and motivation" materials to new distributors is a red flag of fraud or abuse. It is an immediate sign that the manufacturer is deceiving and churning the distributors. The profit gained from the training "tools" depletes the distributors' resources for the real business – selling the manufacturer's goods – and is therefore at odds with the distributors' interests. If this profit is gained without the full knowledge of the distributors, as is true in the Amway distributor business, the abuse is compounded.

Further, if the manufacturer can earn substantial profit from "training" distributors, then the entire business focus is insidiously shifted. The more distributors pay for training, the more profit to the company whether the distributor ever succeeds or not. When the potential profit is large, as in MLM, and can actually exceed profit margins from distributor sales of products, the core business is fundamentally corrupted.

At that point, the business more closely resembles a confidence scheme than a distributor channel. The distributor's trust is gained with deceptive claims of income to be earned from the "independent distribution business" he believes he is investing in. The trust is then used to gain payments for so-called training and other "requirements" for the illusory success he is urged to pursue.[7]

(Robert L. FitzPatrick, E-Mail to author)

Do any of the Seminar/Teaching tools teach people how to market Amway products and services? Just a very few. They carry titles like *The Turtle Won The Race, 2 Pats on the Back for Every Slap on the Wrist, White Shirts and Red Ties, Give It the Heat, Thinking in Multiples of Emerald, Give Up a Little to Get a Lot, Just Like Amway Only Better, Horizontal and Vertical Growth, Free Enterprise Day Speeches,* and *Ring Your Life with Life's Riches.* There is even one video which is categorized as *Tools (Importance of)* which discusses Amway's new Business Support Materials Arbitration Agreement, an insidious contract which we will discuss later.

What about the "attitude" or "commitment" tapes? Their titles are *Undeniable Truths* and *The People You Meet,* and *Storms of Perfection.* The *Next Generation* videos feature the children of high-level achievers in the Yager organization at play: their *Winter Retreat, 1997* and *Yager Youth Leadership Conferences.* This is supposed to demonstrate the wonderful impact the Amway business has on the lives of the distributors' children.

Of the 26 new tapes, books and videos on the December, 1997 list, exactly three, or 11.5% deal with selling products or services. The other 88.5% all promote the use of tools and **plugging into the system!**

The tapes are repetitive: after you've heard a dozen or so teaching tapes, you've pretty much heard all the information they offer. So why subscribe to Standing Order Tape (SOT) and buy a tape per week? Your upline will use circular reasoning to explain: "If you're listening to tapes but you haven't achieved what you want, then obviously you haven't listened to enough tapes. Even if the information sounds repetitive, some day, someone on some tape (or at some function) will say something just a little bit differently, and it will be the missing piece that helps you to build a successful business. You don't want to miss the one thing that will help your business explode, do you?" The solution, if you're not "where you want to be" in the business, is to listen to more tapes, read more books and attend more functions (all sold to you by your upline of course).

You will be told frequently that your AMO leader started offering the tapes, books and functions out of the goodness of his heart, because he realized it would help you **grow** in the business. "He didn't have to invest all that money in a tape duplication facility," you are reminded. "But he did it because he knew how important the tapes are to your growth." Nowhere is it mentioned that he makes any money at all – let alone the vast majority of his income – on sales of tools.

The Rules Have Changed, but for the AMOs it's Business as Usual

Each year, between September 1 and December 31, distributors must renew their distributorships. In September, 1997, Amway began requiring renewing distributors to sign agreements regarding sales of tools, or what Amway calls Business Support Materials (BSMs). The new *Intent to Continue (ITC)* form states: "I understand that the purchase of. . . [BSM] materials is always optional."[8] If a distributor chooses to purchase BSMs, Amway requires him to sign a *Business Support Materials Arbitration Agreement (BSMAA)*.

Your sponsor, according to Amway's rules, is obligated to train and motivate you whether or not you participate in the system. The BSMAA states that neither Amway nor anyone else can require a distributor to purchase BSMs.

> If you sponsor others, you have an obligation to train and motivate them whether or not they choose to buy Business Support Materials. All Distributors are free to change their volume of purchases of such items, to cancel standing orders, or to cease such purchases at any time without threats, pressure, or retaliation.[9]

Sadly, this is **completely** ignored by distributors in the field.

The BSMAA also reminds distributors that, according to Amway's Rules of Conduct, anyone who sells BSMs must buy them back if asked within 180 days of the purchase date. Has it gotten any easier for distributors to return tools and get their money back?

In an e-mail dated April 27, 1998, a disillusioned distributor writes:

> *I still can't believe the amount of money I spent on all of those tools. My sponsor said he'd pay us back for the unopened tapes when he sold them and he'd give us half back for the opened tapes. So [my husband] boxed up a ton of them and I wrote them up. Then they changed their tune....I could only get my money back if the tapes were unopened and I had bought them within the last six months. We decided that the effort and the fight wasn't worth the energy we'd have to put into it...so we cut our losses and dropped it. But I still get mad that he changed his tune.*[10]

On April 5, 1998, another distributor e-mails:

> *Remember how I said I was going to get some money back from the tapes? Well, guess what, I haven't heard a thing from my former Direct.*

He responded to a couple messages of mine, but since then I haven't heard a thing. And now, my messages are not being returned.[11]

Does Amway enforce its own rules? The record of legal complaints against the company clearly indicates that it does not. Regardless of the agreements that you sign, the sad reality is that your upline exerts tremendous pressure on you to buy tools and attend functions, and there is no practical recourse if you later want to recoup your losses unless you're willing to commence lengthy legal battles.

Has your upline ever made statements like, "I don't make any money until I help you become successful"? Using actual sales data from my former employer's business, I discovered that the average distributor (at least, in that particular AMO) represents revenues of about $1,000 per year to his upline from books, tapes, and sponsoring tools alone, **whether or not he ever sponsors a single distributor or sells a single product.** Your upline Direct Distributor keeps a small portion of this $1,000.00. Your upline Diamond keeps substantially more. Obviously your upline has a strong interest in selling you tools!

If we compare the Diamond's income from tools to the Diamond's income from your product use or sales, it becomes quickly obvious why there is such an enormous emphasis on consumption of tools and attendance at functions. Let's assume that your upline qualifies as a Direct Distributor for all 12 months. If you order 100 PV of Amway products personally on a monthly basis, or 2400 PV/4800 BV for the year, you spend about $5424.00 for products. Your upline Direct will get a 25% bonus on that 4800 BV, or about $1200. The Diamond will receive a much smaller piece of those products, somewhere around $264 depending on several variables.

However, income from the tools is reversed. The bonus system for tools is extremely complicated, so there are a great many variables. On the average, though, it's safe to say that of your $1000 tool purchase during the year, your upline Direct will get a bonus of only $120, while your Diamond's cut will be anywhere from $200 to $490. If your Direct has 50 core distributorships in his group, all ordering their 100 PV per month, and purchasing an average number of tools, his income will be about $15,000 from product movement, and $6,000 from tools for that group during the year. On the same group volume of products vs. tools, the Diamond will earn about $6,000 from products and $24,500 from tools. This demonstrates why your upline, as he moves up from one pin level to another, changes his emphasis from promoting product flow to promoting tool consumption.

Jeff Probandt is an Emerald Direct Distributor who has publicized some of the abuses of the AMO system on a website. He describes on his website the conversation he had with his upline when he first qualified as a Direct Distributor.

> "Well, Jeff, you've been working very hard to go Direct. (I was 19 at the time, and of course I wholeheartedly agreed!) You've put a lot of miles on your car, bought a lot of tools, many of which you gave out and didn't get back. (Yes, this was all true.) We have a way to help compensate you for all that called "tape breaks". (At this point I was moving about 500 to 750 tapes a month through my organization.) Tapes cost (at that time) $5 a piece. We are going to give you 20 cents per tape as a bonus to help make up for some of the expenses you've had." He went on to tell me that Dexter Yager put money in the system to make up for the fact that there wasn't enough money in the Amway® plan. He told me that this was a secret that you only found out about when you went Direct. I wasn't to tell anyone. He told me this tape break was not a right but a privilege. This money should not be used to create a lifestyle but to help me give away more tapes and put gas in my car. It was implied that if I were ever not building the business, this "tape break" money would be taken away.
>
> As I am writing this, it seems so obvious to me that the "tape break" was wrong. I didn't see it that way at the time. The people in my upline had been so edified (deified) that I'm sure there wasn't much they could have told me that I would have questioned.[12] (Probandt, internet)

Probandt outlined the "tape break" for each level that he personally achieved, from raw distributor up through Emerald with two Emeralds in depth. A distributor pays $6.00 per tape in that organization. The Direct pays only $5.70, a Sapphire $5.45, an Emerald $5.20, and an Emerald with two Emeralds in depth, $4.95. Probandt claims that at the Emerald Direct Distributor level, abut half the income is from the system. My experience supports this. And of course, the Diamond's ratio of Amway/system income is much more lopsided.

In another organization, the tape bonuses were handled differently. Instead of the "tape break" where a Direct actually paid less for tapes than he sold them for, a complicated system of bonuses and refunds was in place. Like the BV on Amway products, each tool had a value, called CV, placed on it by InterNET Services Corp. or the AMO leader who produced it. Directs, Pearls, Sapphires, Emeralds and Diamonds earned bonuses based on this CV. A tape which sold for $6.00 carried a CV of 5.55. This CV represented the profit which would be shared out. The Direct would get 12% (67 cents), the Emerald 33% ($1.83), the first Diamond 49% ($2.72), and the remaining 51% ($3.28) was divided among other upline Diamonds and Yager.

If you're quick at math, you've realized that this adds up to more than 100%. The tool bonuses follow the line of sponsorship, and money comes from the top down. In other words, the Diamond gets a check from his upline or from InterNET Services Corp. for 49% of his CV. Out of this, he must pay his qualified Emeralds and Directs. If he's a qualified Diamond, with three Emerald and three Direct legs, he keeps 16% of the CV bonus on each Emerald leg and 37% on each Direct leg.

Contrast this with the bonuses for Amway product purchases, which cap at 27% for Directs and are just a fraction of a percent for Sapphires, Emeralds and Diamonds and you'll begin to see why the AMO leaders promote the tools so strongly.

SIX: What Is the "System"?

The "system," in AMO parlance, refers to the use of tools discussed in Chapter Three, and to all the functions created by the AMO organization. The functions include:

1. Introductory Seminars, or Open Meetings
2. Seminars & Rallies
3. Major functions with names like Free Enterprise Day, Fall Extravaganza, Dream Weekend, Leadership, Go Diamond, Weekend of the Diamonds, Family Reunion, Summer Conference and Winter Conference.

Introductory Seminars

An Introductory Seminar, or Open Meeting, is a meeting held in a public place like a hotel or restaurant meeting room. Distributors in a particular line of sponsorship come, along with their prospects, to see someone (who is at least a Direct Distributor) show the plan. All active distributors are encouraged (AMO-speak for *pressured*) to attend, whether or not they have a prospect to bring, in order to support the system. If the distributorship is a husband and wife couple, as about 80% are, both are expected to attend. There is an admission charge for the

Introductory Seminar, of course; up to $6.00 per person in some AMOs. So a distributor husband and wife would pay up to $12.00. Prospects are admitted at no charge. Some AMOs will accept checks to cover the admission cost, but most discourage this and some accept cash only. No receipts are given, so attending distributors will not have proof of this business expense. Nor will the leaders keep records of what they take in.

Distributors are taught to bring their new prospects to the speaker following the meeting and introduce him. A typical introduction goes something like this:

"Hi Dave Direct, this is Pete and Pam Prospect! Pete's flat turned on about this business. He really wants to get his wife home from her job, and he'd like to have a boat. Pete, Dave has been tearing this thing up. He's a real winner, and we're lucky to have him here tonight."

In turn, Dave Direct knows his lines. After chatting with Pete for a minute or two about what kind of boat he'd like to have, Dave will say, "Pete, you need to get back together with Sam Sponsor here. Sam's a real winner, and he's become a wonderful student of this business. You can't do any better than tie in with him. You need to set up a time to get back together with Sam so he can show the plan to some of your prospects. Have you made your list yet? No? Well, there's a tape you need to get. . ."

Pete still has a lot of questions, and he's really not sure he wants to get involved. But he doesn't want to disappoint Sam, who believes he's excited, and after all, Sam's a real winner who can help Pete succeed! Naturally, Dave doesn't tell Pete that he has never met Sam before. Or, if he actually does know Sam, he won't tell Pete that Sam has been involved in the business for a year and never received a bonus check. They act all buddy-buddy, and Pete leaves thinking that his sponsor-to-be is really achieving great things in the Amway business, and can help him do the same.

After the Introductory Seminar, typically, the **winners** in the group, those who are **sharp** and **motivated,** will go to a local coffee shop for an **after meeting.** When Dave Direct enters the restaurant, most of his group will already be there, and they'll clap and cheer when he walks in the door. Someone will make sure he gets waited on right away, ahead of the rest who've been waiting longer. He will ostentatiously loosen his tie. He'll sit at a table carefully reserved for him by the Direct Distributor who arranged the location for the after-meeting. Distributors and prospects in ones and twos will come and visit him at his table. He'll dispense information, compliments, and attaboys and everyone will leave feeling edified and uplifted. It's wonderful to be around such positive people!

If you attend the Introductory Seminar, you pay an admission charge, usually $10-12 per couple. If you're an "average" distributor, you probably paid for a babysitter. You paid $40 for a tape pack that Dave told you would help you. And coffee afterwards was another $10.00 because you didn't have dinner before the meeting (no time!), so you split an order of nachos and left a big tip to impress the waitress you tried to prospect. Isn't it wonderful to be able to spend time with such positive people!

Seminars & Rallies

The Seminar & Rally is a monthly event in most AMOs. The Seminar takes place on a Saturday afternoon and the Rally on Saturday evening. Some months there will also be a Leadership on Friday night, which distributors must qualify to attend. The speakers are usually the same for each session. Typically, the speakers will be a couple at the Pearl (recently changed to Sapphire) or Emerald level; occasionally, speakers will be Direct Distributors and there will be no Friday night Leadership. Different AMOs handle admission differently. Some have separate tickets for the Saturday afternoon seminar and the Saturday evening rally, some combine the admission on one ticket. Admission will range from $10-20 for the day, per person. Prospects as well as distributors pay full ticket price. The Leaderships are usually handled the same as the Introductory Seminars; in many organization, each attendee pays cash at the door and no records are kept.

To qualify for attendance at the Leadership meeting, the distributor must either have reached the 12% Performance Bonus level at some time, or meet fast-growth qualifications determined by his AMO. Leaderships, depending on how many attend, are usually held in the same sorts of meeting rooms as the Introductory Seminars. Admission will be $5-10 at the door, about half the price of the Seminar & Rally. Sometimes the Leadership meeting serves as a warmup for the speakers for their seminar the following day, and distributors hear the same information twice. Occasionally the same information will be presented, but in a more straightforward fashion at the Leadership. Rarely will the speakers present anything at the Leadership that isn't repeated at the next day's seminar. But, if you qualify to go, you're expected to be there. After all, you have to support the system!

At the Seminar, the speakers will "teach the basics" of building a successful Amway business. Some of these basics include discussions of proper dress, the husband's role, the wife's role, the importance of tools, how to have a successful meeting, how to **motivate** your kids so they don't mind you leaving them with babysitters all the time, how to answer your telephone, how to clean your house, and frequently how you should conduct your spiritual life and marital relationship! No subject is too sacred for advice from these speakers.

The Rally is the "fun" part of the function. This is where the speakers talk about their own experience with the Amway business, what their lives were like before they saw the plan, and all the material goodies they have now. They dress formally, in long gowns and conservative suits or occasionally tuxedos, and flaunt expensive jewelry and furs. There is generally a lot of laughter, and sometimes a few tears. Of course, they have to keep it positive! Speakers are allowed to discuss some of the negative things that happened to them "before the business," and they're allowed to talk about the struggles they've had with negative (former) friends and family. They are **not** allowed to discuss anything negative about the business, their line of sponsorship, or their downline. They can discuss their accomplishments in the business, but they can't tell the audience that when they were recognized as new Direct Distributors, they had $50,000 charged to their credit cards for business-related travel and tools, and that they have no idea how they'll pay it off. They can discuss all the wonderful **friendships** they've developed in the business, but they can't admit that their teenager is skipping school, drinking, and has cracked up the car three times in the past year.

At the end of the Rally, all of the Direct Distributors are called up on stage, and the evening ends with everyone joining hands and singing *God Bless America*. Usually there is a receiving line for the speakers. In some organizations, the banners that decorated the meeting room are taken down, and attending distributors sign them and express their appreciation to the speakers for the great job that they did. Afterwards, the **winners** will meet at a local restaurant for coffee and snacks, and a chance – if you're lucky – to talk to the speakers in person. If the speakers are Emeralds or Diamonds, they will let you try on their jewelry. "Oh, that ring looks wonderful on your hand. You really deserve to have something nice like this, and if you just keep doing what you're doing, you'll be successful and you can have one of your own!" Back in the early 1980's when I was first involved, I used to hear expressions like, "Honey, if you just move enough SA-8™ (Amway's laundry product), your hands will break out in diamonds," but with zero emphasis today on selling product, that expression has disappeared.

Distributors are told over and over again at functions and on the tapes that the mark of a winner, is to be "the first one to arrive and the last one to leave." So some of the winners won't leave the restaurant until 1:00 or 2:00 AM. A "normal" travel time to a monthly Seminar & Rally can be up to three hours (I used to go six or seven hours away), so if you leave the restaurant at 1:00 and live three hours away, you get home at 4:00 AM. I'm excited, how 'bout you? Isn't it great to be around such positive people?

Major Functions

Each Diamond AMO will host three or four major functions each year, and will combine with upline for several more. Typically a Diamond will hold some sort of a summer function, a winter function, one in the fall and another in the spring. The summer function used to be known as Family Reunion, where all the distributors in that Diamond "family" would get together in one place. Some now are calling them "Summer Conferences" or "Summer Workshops," as they feel the name change makes it easier for their distributors to get a tax deduction for their expenses of attendance. These used to always be held on the Fourth of July weekend, but many Diamond AMOs are so large now that they must choose other dates so as not to conflict with their upline or downline Diamond's functions. (This way they can all speak at each other's functions, and collect hefty **honorariums**.) For the average distributor, the Summer Conference will run from Friday evening to Saturday evening, although the winners will be sure to attend the non-denominational Christian worship service on Sunday morning, and the leaders will attend the afternoon Leadership meeting. Typically, those at the Direct Distributor level will have their own meeting on Thursday night prior to the start of the conference; higher-level Sapphire and Emerald pins will meet on the Wednesday preceding the weekend.

The winter function used to be called *Dream Weekend* or *Dream Night*; again, some Diamond AMOs are now calling them Winter Conferences or Winter Workshops. According to stories, Dream Night was started by the Downeast organization, a coalition of three distributorships headed by Don and Nancy Wilson, Tim and Sherri Bryan, and Tedd and Naomi Fish, all of Maine at that time. The first Dream Night was held as a **positive** alternative to the traditional New Year's Eve party. At this function, luxury cars were brought into the hall, and jewelers, furriers, and real estate agents were invited in to display their wares and sell to distributors. Eventually, Dream Night became a standard in the Yager AMO repertoire, and expanded to fill a whole weekend instead of just an evening. Because of the size and number of Diamond AMOs holding these functions, dates are spread out through December and January. Some organizations will even hold Dream Night during Christmas week.

Extravaganzas or Diamond Rallies are similar to the monthly Seminar & Rally in all but size. The Diamond AMO will choose one or a few centralized locations and bring large numbers of distributors together for a weekend featuring several Diamond speakers. There will usually be a Leadership on Friday night, or possibly on Sunday afternoon. Diamond Rallies are often scheduled on or near Easter and Thanksgiving.

Often the Diamond AMO will hold a special Leadership session featuring one of the "big" AMO leaders like Yager or Britt. This will be a Friday night and all day Saturday function, and you will be rigorously pressured to qualify to attend, even to the extent of "buying" your qualification by purchasing thousands of dollars worth of Amway product. Ticket prices to these functions are in the $50-75 range. Some organizations require you to buy their **package**, which includes and hotel and some meals. This will generally cost about $275-400.

The biggest AMO leaders hold several additional functions each year. The most well-known of these is Dexter Yager's **Free Enterprise Day Celebration.** Originally held in Charlotte, NC, on Labor Day Weekend, the organization has expanded so much that Yager holds several events each year, in locations throughout the US and Canada. Each of these will be attended by anywhere from 20,000 to 100,000 distributors, depending on the location. Distributors who have reached Diamond status for the first time will speak, and usually Yager will bring in a well-known conservative political figure, and some professional entertainment as well.

Free Enterprise includes sessions on Friday evening, Saturday all day and night, with a non-denominational Christian worship service on Sunday morning. Additionally, on the Thursday prior to the weekend there will be a session for Direct Distributors and above, with special meetings in advance for the Emeralds and Diamonds as well. Cost for the Direct Distributors meeting is usually $10 per person, in cash, with no receipts given.

I used to drive about 18 hours to attend Free Enterprise Day in Charlotte, NC. The Friday evening session would start at 7:00 PM and run until about 1:00 or 2:00 AM. (The reason we were let out so "early" was because the leaders realized that most of us had been on the road all day.) In order to be there by starting time, I would either take two days for the trip, stopping with relatives halfway and spending the night, or leave home about midnight and drive straight through. Some distributors from Canada would drive for 36 hours straight to arrive in Charlotte by the starting time. Saturday morning the sessions would start again about 9:00 AM and go until about 5:00 with no breaks. We would have a brief dinner break, then go back in about 7:00 and run until "Dex," who always wrapped up the evening, got tired of talking, often well after 3:00 AM. Sunday morning at 10:00 would see the coliseum filled again for the worship service. Few people would really eat meals during the weekend, instead subsisting on snacks of nachos or hot dogs from the concession stands, along with gallons of coffee and soft drinks.

Those distributors who are winners and "serious" stay glued to their seats throughout the entire function. After all, if you get up and walk around, or leave early, you might miss the one important statement that can propel you to Diamond! One year, by Saturday night I was so exhausted and strung out from bad food that I became nauseous, and had to leave before the Yagers came on. It wasn't yet 2:00 AM, I had probably had about eight hours sleep in three days, but because I was leaving early I was showing the AMO world that I was not a winner.

On the annual Yager calendar there is also Go Diamond Weekend, for Silvers and Up, which is held in one location for all North American distributors; and Weekend of the Diamonds.

Let's just take a look at this AMO calendar for a moment. We'll follow Amway's fiscal year, which begins in September.

* Labor Day Weekend is when Free Enterprise Day (actually an entire weekend) is traditionally held.

Ticket prices range from about $80-100 per person. In 1997, Yager/InterNET held Free Enterprise in six North American locations: Boston, MA; Charlotte, NC; San Diego, CA; Houston, TX; St. Louis, MO; and Toronto, Canada. However, because of the unique way the system works, the majority of people must travel very long distances to attend. Logically, those who live in New England would attend the Boston function, those in the upper Midwest and Canada would attend Toronto, and so on. However, function attendance is based on lines of sponsorship. Therefore, if you happen to live in Toronto but your upline Diamond's organization is centered in the Southeastern United States, you would attend the Charlotte, NC function. If you live in Los Angeles but your Diamond AMO is centered in New England, you get to go to Boston! InterNET simply will not make the San Diego tickets available in your group. We will discuss the reasoning behind this later.[1]

- Thanksgiving. **Fall Extravaganza** or **Diamond Rally** is usually held on or close to Thanksgiving weekend. Tickets for these weekends can range from about $40-90 per person. Most distributors won't have to drive more than six to eight hours to attend these functions, unlike Free Enterprise where you can easily travel across the country.

- Christmas or New Year's Eve. **Dream Weekend** or **Winter Conference/Workshop.** Tickets will sell for $90-125 per person; many AMOs, put together a package deal which includes the hotel room and some meals and can cost over $400. Distributors who live in the local area and don't need the hotel room will still have to pay the package price. Travel for this function can be extensive, as each Diamond AMO will typically have just one function in one centralized location.

- Easter. **Spring Extravaganza** or **Diamond Rally.** Same as Fall Extravaganza, about $40-90 per person. Also, for those who qualify, Go Diamond Weekend. For the past few years, this function has been held in Florida. Ticket prices in 1998 ran from $90 to $100 depending on how far in advance the tickets were purchased, with an additional $100 for the Emerald Leadership.

- Fourth of July. **Family Reunion** or **Summer Conference/Workshop.** Usually $90-110 per person, sometimes as part of a package including hotel and some meals. A package including two nights hotel, two breakfasts, and a banquet on Saturday night can cost over $500 per couple. This function can also involve extensive travel, as the goal for Family Reunion is to bring all the distributors in a single Diamond AMO together in one location. It is not unusual for distributors to travel literally from one end of the country to the other to attend; in Diamond AMOs where international growth is taking place, foreign distributors are strongly encouraged to attend their upline North American Diamond's Family Reunion. I have met distributors from at least six foreign countries at these functions in my former AMO.

Anyone who is serious about building the business will attend all of these, as well as the monthly Seminars & Rallies and Introductory Seminars. Some AMO organizations will omit the monthly Seminar & Rally during months when there is a major function; some hold – and insist on attendance at – both.

Miscellaneous Functions

There are usually a few functions that fall into the "miscellaneous" category: special **Nuts and Bolts** sessions, and sessions just for the men or just for the women. Prices on these will vary tremendously.

SEVEN: What Does the "System" Cost?

I Get Started in the System

In Chapter Two I recounted how I got started in the Amway business. Sally Sponsor, and our upline Steve Silver, sponsored me by the book, and brought me into the motivational system equally smoothly.

Steve explains the system to me this way: Our upline Crown Ambassador (then Triple Diamond), Dexter Yager, has discovered that we distributors need to be nourished with positive information to counteract all the negative that is out there in the real world of selling products and sponsoring people. So, in his great wisdom, Dexter started the system where we can purchase motivational and informational tapes and books at a reasonable cost. Success in the Amway business is built on a foundation of tapes, books and functions. The tapes provide information and inspiration about the Amway business. In order to keep our attitudes positive, we need to listen to a minimum of one tape each day.

Books serve a different purpose, Steve explains. According to motivational speaker and author Charlie "Tremendous" Jones, "where you will be in five years is determined by the books you read and the people you associate with." It's vital to read the right books. Therefore, you must also stop reading the "wrong" books. The only books you should read are those you purchase through the system. Stop reading novels, mysteries, romances, history, philosophy, anything but positive (i.e., system) books. The books available through the system at this time are limited. Paul Conn had written *Believe!* (Berkley Publishing), *The Possible Dream* (Berkley Publishing) and *The Winner's Circle* (Berkley Publishing). Robert Schuller and Norman Vincent Peale have several books that the system has put its stamp of approval on, but there aren't too many more. I'm a book-a-day reader, so finding "approved" daily reading becomes a real challenge for me. (In the Amway business, we don't have "problems" any more, we have "challenges.") Today there are hundreds of "approved" books promoted and sold by the AMO systems.

It is vitally important to attend every Open Meeting. (We call them Introductory Seminars today.) Even if we don't have a prospect, we should go ourselves to support our upline who is sacrificing to make these opportunities available to us. The closest Open Meetings for me are at least a one-hour drive away, but I need to put them all on my calendar.

Seminar & Rally is a monthly event, and if I'm going to be successful in my new business, I must attend every one without fail. I need this monthly injection of positive to "keep my attitude right" so I can build the business.

There are also major functions three times each year, and I must attend those in order to succeed in the business. In fact, Spring Extravaganza is coming up next month. It's only 300 miles away, and I need to make my reservations quickly as it is almost sold out. It's going to be exciting! There will be hundreds of distributors there, and the speakers will be Diamonds! It will accelerate my business growth by six months to a year. In my only independent stand early in my Amway career, I tell Steve I cannot possibly attend this function. I have no money, and I have a nursing baby to take care of. Although he aggressively promotes this function each time he talks with me in the ensuing month, I stand my ground and I do not attend Spring Extravaganza. Because later I feel so guilty at missing this important function, it is the *only* major function I miss for years.

To participate fully in the system, I have to switch over from whatever products I've been buying to purely Amway products. Household cleaning products, vitamins, makeup, personal care items, all must wear the Amway label. If it's order day and there is nothing I need, I should order something anyway. Get a product to try – if I haven't used it myself, how can I sell it?

Within my first few weeks in the Amway business, I purchase an Amway Sales & Product Kit; a dozen tapes; four books; and a Seminar & Rally ticket. I pay a babysitter four or five times, and drive about 500 business miles. I purchase products in addition to those that come in the kit. Altogether I spend about $400. At the end of the month, I get a Performance Bonus check for three dollars and change. I have two children to support, and huge legal fees for my divorce, which my husband is inexplicably fighting.

Steve invites me to come and have Sunday dinner with his family. I drive to the house, and Steve meets me outside and gives me an enormous hug. I wonder about Steve's motivation in helping me with my business. I go upstairs, and Sarah greets me with a hug also. I had been expecting a leisurely, relaxed meal. But no, Steve and Sarah have a meeting scheduled at 4:00, so we'll eat at 2:00 and that will give them time to get to their meeting. It's clear to me by the time I leave that if I want time with Steve and Sarah, I will have to build a big business and make it worth their while. Before I leave, each of them gives me a big hug again. Since the hug from Steve this time is in front of Sarah, and she obviously doesn't mind, I realize it's just an Amway thing. They are such nice people, obviously warm and caring. Sarah has a wonderful sense of humor, and their kids are outgoing and happy. I decide I want to spend more time with people like this.

> "Build the friendship, and the Directship will follow."
>
> Dexter Yager
>
> Relationships develop out of friendships, and enough close relationships build Directships... one of the best ways to begin cementing your relationships with your distributors is by realizing that you must set the example in... building enough... friendships to permit you to go Direct.[1]
>
> (Yager, p. 310)

Then and Now

There are some minor differences in the system between the early 1980's, when I first became involved, and today. Back then, the tapes that were moved through the system came unwrapped and it was very common for the same tape to be sold and resold five or six times. A

Function Expenses, 1996
Excluding Leaderships

MONTH	NAME OF FUNCTION	INITIAL COST OF TICKET	FIRST COST INCREASE	COST AT DOOR	AVERAGE COST	AVERAGE COST PER COUPLE
January	Winter Conference/ Dream Weekend	$ 115.00	$ 120.00	$ 120.00	$ 118.33	$236.67
	Introductory Seminar*	10.00	10.00	10.00	10.00	20.00
February	Seminar and Rally	12.00	12.00	15.00	13.00	26.00
	Miscellanous: Ladies Artistry Training	30.00	30.00	30.00	30.00	30.00
	Introductory Seminar	10.00	10.00	10.00	10.00	20.00
March	Yager Go Diamond	85.00	90.00	90.00	88.33	176.67
	Diamond Rally	52.00	52.00	52.00	52.00	104.00
	Introductory Seminar	10.00	10.00	10.00	10.00	20.00
April	Seminar and Rally	12.00	12.00	15.00	13.00	26.00
	Introductory Seminar	10.00	10.00	10.00	10.00	20.00
May	Seminar and Rally	12.00	12.00	15.00	13.00	26.00
	Miscellaneous: Nuts & Bolts	22.00	22.00	22.00	22.00	44.00
	Introductory Seminar	10.00	10.00	10.00	10.00	20.00
June	Seminar and Rally	12.00	12.00	15.00	13.00	26.00
	Introductory Seminar	10.00	10.00	10.00	10.00	20.00

Table 4

distributor could purchase a tape, listen to it, then move it along to some-body in his group and recoup what he'd spent. Today, tapes come shrink-wrapped, and distributors are not allowed to sell unwrapped tapes. Therefore, once a distributor buys a tape he must either keep it, give it away, or throw it away. There is no question of recouping his investment in that tape. Some of the books I purchased through the system in the early days of my distributorship were already dog-eared and highlighted. Today, books passing through the system must be in new condition. When I asked why I was getting used materials, I was told, "you're paying for the

Function Expenses, 1996
Excluding Leaderships

July	Summer Conference/ Family Reunion	100.00	110.00	110.00	106.67	213.33
	Introductory Seminar	10.00	10.00	10.00	10.00	20.00
August	Seminar and Rally	12.00	12.00	15.00	13.00	26.00
	Free Enterprise Day	75.00	80.00	85.00	80.00	160.00
	Introductory Seminar	10.00	10.00	10.00	10.00	20.00
September	Seminar and Rally	12.00	12.00	15.00	13.00	26.00
	Introductory Seminar	10.00	10.00	10.00	10.00	20.00
October	Seminar and Rally	12.00	12.00	15.00	13.00	26.00
	Introductory Seminar	10.00	10.00	10.00	10.00	20.00
November	Fall Extravaganza/ Diamond Rally	50.00	60.00	60.00	56.67	113.33
	Introductory Seminar	10.00	10.00	10.00	10.00	20.00
December	Seminar and Rally	12.00	12.00	15.00	13.00	26.00
	Introductory Seminar	10.00	10.00	10.00	10.00	20.00
TOTAL		745.00	780.00	809.00	778.00	1526.0.00

* Many organizations expect distributors to attend Introductory Seminars on a weekly basis. We have shown attendance only twice each month.

Table 4

information that's inside, not for the condition of the cover." I have no idea what the actual numbers are, but the AMO leaders sell hundreds of thousands more tapes and books each year by forcing distributors to move only "new" items.

Back then, we were encouraged to purchase a tape every week, but there was no organized Standing Order Tape system as there is today. In fact, sometimes the weekly tapes would be different for each member of a group, depending on which tapes the upline wanted to get rid of, or if he thought individual people needed some special training or inspiration in a particular area! Today the SOT selection is made by the umbrella AMO and is consistent throughout the organization.

And, of course, prices have gone up. When I first got involved in the Amway business, a tape cost $3.00, and a ticket for Seminar & Rally was $6.00. Today, in the same organization, tapes are $6.00 and tickets are $12.00 in advance or $15.00 at the door. Tickets for major functions have gone up much more. My first Free Enterprise Day ticket cost me $30.00. Today they run up to $100.00.

What Does the System Cost?

The average North American distributorship is owned by a husband and wife building the business together as a couple. Therefore, we will discuss costs in terms of both husband and wife attending meetings and functions, since this is what the system aggressively promotes. The costs outlined here will not include costs of travel, hotels, meals, and babysitters, which are significant for most distributor couples.

For purposes of illustration, we are using an actual function calendar from one particular AMO, and that organization's ticket prices from calendar year 1996, the most recent full year for which we have information. This illustration presumes that the distributors are core, that is, they follow their upline's recommendation and both attend each and every function that they qualify to attend. Some organizations hold Introductory Seminars only once a month; others have one per week. We are using two Introductory Seminars per month as the average. The larger functions – Dream Weekend, Family Reunion, Free Enterprise, Day, and a few others – have introduced a system of graduated prices for tickets. To encourage distributors to purchase tickets when they first become available, the initial ticket price is lower. There may be one or two increases in tickets before the function actually begins. Since tickets are nonrefundable, the AMO usually sells quite a few extra tickets this way. Where the ticket prices increase, we are using the average to determine the distributor's annual cost.

For the distributor who has not yet achieved a leadership position, the annual cost of admission to functions would be nearly $1,500.00. The cost jumps to $1632.00 for the non-Ddirect couple in a leadership position. For the Direct Distributor couple, the cost increases to over $1800.00. Emeralds and Sapphires pay a lot more to attend their special

Function Expenses, 1996
Including Leaderships

MONTH	NAME OF FUNCTION	INITIAL COST OF TICKET	FIRST COST INCREASE	COST AT DOOR	AVERAGE COST	AVERAGE COST PER COUPLE
January	Winter Conference/ Dream Weekend	$ 115.00	$ 120.00	$ 120.00	$ 118.33	$236.67
	Leadership Meeting	5.00	5.00	5.00	5.00	10.00
	Introductory Seminar*	10.00	10.00	10.00	10.00	20.00
February	Seminar and Rally	12.00	12.00	15.00	13.00	26.00
	With Leadership	6.00	6.00	6.00	6.00	12.00
	Miscellanous: Ladies Artistry Training	30.00	30.00	30.00	30.00	30.00
	Special Leadership	65.00	65.00	65.00	65.00	130.00
	Introductory Seminar	10.00	10.00	10.00	10.00	20.00
March	Yager Go Diamond	85.00	90.00	90.00	88.33	176.67
	Emerald Club	100.00	100.00	100.00	100.00	200.00
	Diamond Rally	52.00	52.00	52.00	52.00	104.00
	Introductory Seminar	10.00	10.00	10.00	10.00	20.00
April	Seminar and Rally	12.00	12.00	15.00	13.00	26.00
	With Leadership	6.00	6.00	6.00	6.00	12.00
	Introductory Seminar	10.00	10.00	10.00	10.00	20.00
May	Seminar and Rally	12.00	12.00	15.00	13.00	26.00
	With Leadership	6.00	6.00	6.00	6.00	12.00
	Miscellaneous: Nuts & Bolts	22.00	22.00	22.00	22.00	44.00
	Introductory Seminar	10.00	10.00	10.00	10.00	20.00
June	Seminar and Rally	12.00	12.00	15.00	13.00	26.00
	With Leadership	6.00	6.00	6.00	6.00	12.00
	Introductory Seminar	10.00	10.00	10.00	10.00	20.00

Table 5

Function Expenses, 1996
Including Leaderships

July	Summer Conference/ Family Reunion	100.00	110.00	110.00	106.67	213.33
	Leadership Meeting	5.00	5.00	5.00	5.00	10.00
	Introductory Seminar	10.00	10.00	10.00	10.00	20.00
August	Seminar and Rally	12.00	12.00	15.00	13.00	26.00
	With Leadership	6.00	6.00	6.00	6.00	12.00
	Free Enterprise Day	75.00	80.00	85.00	80.00	160.00
	Direct Distributor Leadership	10.00	10.00	10.00	10.00	20.00
	Emerald Leadership	30.00	30.00	30.00	30.00	60.00
	Introductory Seminar	10.00	10.00	10.00	10.00	20.00
September	Seminar and Rally	12.00	12.00	15.00	13.00	26.00
	Introductory Seminar	10.00	10.00	10.00	10.00	20.00
October	Seminar and Rally	12.00	12.00	15.00	13.00	26.00
	With Leadership	6.00	6.00	6.00	6.00	12.00
	Introductory Seminar	10.00	10.00	10.00	10.00	20.00
November	Fall Extravaganza/ Diamond Rally	50.00	60.00	60.00	56.67	113.33
	Leadership Meeting	5.00	5.00	5.00	5.00	10.00
	Introductory Seminar	10.00	10.00	10.00	10.00	20.00
December	Seminar and Rally	12.00	12.00	15.00	13.00	26.00
	With Leadership	6.00	6.00	6.00	6.00	12.00
	Introductory Seminar	10.00	10.00	10.00	10.00	20.00
TOTAL		1007.00	1042.00	1071.00	1040.00	2050.00

* Many organizations expect distributors to attend Introductory Seminars on a weekly basis. We have shown attendance only twice each month.

Table 5

"clubs" and other required meetings sponsored by their upline AMO. Diamonds have additional meetings they attend and pay for.

Tape and book purchases involve more variables. A distributor who is prospecting more, showing more plans, and sponsoring more people will generally be buying more tools than the average. While the backbone of the tool business is the weekly Standing Order Tape, the tool catalog includes hundreds of other items that can be purchased. Some are recommended for use in prospecting, or immediately after showing the plan, after the followup, or for general motivation at any time. It is expected that distributors will lose, give away, or

Average Annual Tool Purchases, per Active Distributor on Startup			
Item Purchased	Average Units Purchased	Price per Unit	Total Price
SOT	52	$ 6.00	$ 312.00
PaceSetter	26	6.00	156.00
BOM	6	12.95	77.70
VOM	6	16.00	96.00
Tool Box	2	60.00	120.00
First Night Pack	4	36.00	144.00
Second Night Pack	3	60.00	180.00
Profiles of Success	1	30.00	30.00
Board and Easel with Accessories*	1	100.00	100.00
Contacting Tapes	10	6.00	60.00
Ad Packs	10	7.00	70.00
DBR Tapes	10	6.00	60.00
Literature/Sales Aids			25.00
Teaching Videos	3	16.50	49.50
Contacting Videos	2	16.50	33.00
Special/Lifestyle Videos	4	16.50	66.00
Computer Software	1	149.00	149.00
TOTAL			1728.20

* Usually a one- time purchase

Table 6

loan and fail to get back a certain number of tools. Some AMO leaders promote purchasing enormous quantities of prospecting and sponsoring tapes. I have heard one Diamond claim that if a distributor doesn't have at least 100 generic tapes for use in prospecting, he is not serious about building the business. "Don't worry about getting them back," this Diamond advises. "It's not worth your time to go chasing all over trying to get back one little tape. Your time is worth more than the tape is, just replace it." (Once we know how much bonus money the Diamond makes on your tape purchases, this advice becomes a lot more understandable!) That's an investment of $600 or more, depending on your AMO organization, in tools that you expect to lose and replace. We have compiled a list of what an "average" distributor might purchase during the course of a year.

Looking at these figures, then, with average expenses for tools and functions, an average couple can expect to spend about $3200.00 per year for tools and admission to functions. Our estimate of the actual cost of function attendance, including estimates for hotels, meals, and babysitters, jumps that figure up to nearly $7,500.00 each year. (And remember, this does not include the cost of travel to the functions.) This means that, according to Amway's example in the *SA4400*, you need to be in the 18% Performance Bonus bracket with a group structured like their example, just to pay for your tools and functions. How many distributors reach the 18% bracket? No data are available, but it's unlikely to be more than five percent of all distributors, and is most probably less.

Most distributors who have shared this information with me claim to have lost between $5-8,000 per year during the years they were involved in Amway. Jeff and Joni Probandt are Emerald Direct Distributors. In an unusually courageous move, the Probandts opened a site on the World Wide Web in March of 1998, where they lay out the financial facts of their personal business. Probandt conservatively estimates the costs of being core at about $9,684 per year. His figures includes SOT, Go Getter Tape (the same as PaceSetter), other tools, Introductory Seminars, Seminars & Rallies, major functions, and transportation to functions (but not babysitters or food and beverage costs). The Probandts are part of the InterNET AMO, through Crown Direct Distributor Ken Stewart's line of sponsorship.

In the next chapter, we will take a close look at who benefits from these distributor expenditures.

EIGHT: Show Me The Money

Amway Income and Expenses

The Amway business is always presented as a way to make money – lots and lots of money! The Sales and Marketing Plan, as demonstrated in Amway's *SA4400* shows you, at the Direct Distributor level, earning $25,656.00 per year. If you continue to qualify as a Direct, with a monthly PV of 7,900 and you also sponsor a Direct Distributor with the same volume, you'll receive an additional $632.00 per month as a Leadership Bonus, for an annual income of $33,480.00. This is *not* a large income. Besides, how many Direct Distributors actually earn this income? Amway won't release those figures. However, Amway does admit that only one out of every 45 active distributors actually sees these incomes in any *single* month during the year, and the *average* Direct's Performance Bonus during 1995 was only $1,352.00. Annualized, that would be $16,224.00 per year.

When you subtract the estimated $1,000.00 per year spent on tools by an average distributor – for a Direct it would be more – and the cost of function tickets ($1790.00 at the Direct Distributor level), profit is reduced to about $13,434.00. If you include our estimates for the real cost of attending functions, including meals and babysitters (but not travel) that figure is further reduced to $7,468.00.* And you still have to pay for for your telephone and Amvox, gas for the car when you show the plan, meals out and babysitters when you show the plan, additional clothing expenses in some cases, the products you're personally using (at a premium of about 40% over what you would pay for comparable products at the store) and any other expenses associated with building an Amway distributorship. The Wisconsin Attorney General did a study, and found an average *net loss* of $918.00 per year for a Direct Distributor.

If you took the same number of hours, 2875.5 per year according to our estimate, that you spend with your Amway business, and took a minimum wage job, you would earn $15,096.00 without any of those associated expenses except perhaps the babysitter and gas for your car.

Any *real money* at all in Amway is to be found at the Emerald and Diamond levels. But first you have to get there.

Going Direct

The first major level to achieve is Silver Producer (see Figure 1). This means you've reached a group volume of 7500 PV in any single month, placing you in the 25% Performance Bonus bracket. Maintain this for three months and you're a Gold Producer; for six months out of the fiscal year, and you're a Direct Distributor, or Gold Direct. If you maintain it for all twelve months, you're a Founders Direct Distributor. The Amway Sales and Marketing Plan shows a Direct Distributor sponsoring six legs, each of whom sponsors four, each of whom sponsors two. They each generate 100 PV per month, for a total PV of 7800. After paying out bonuses according to this example, you are left with about $2000. In real life, it doesn't ever happen like that, and the income isn't nearly that much.

The most common configuration for a new Silver Producer is one very strong leg, with one or two small legs. There may also be a handful of

---

*   Probandt, on his website, claims annual average expenses, *excluding* the purchase of Amway products and services, at $9,684. Jeff Probandt, *An In-Depth Look At The Amway Business*, 23 Mar. 1998 <http://209.196.24.186/system.htm>.

Amway's Representation of a Silver Producer

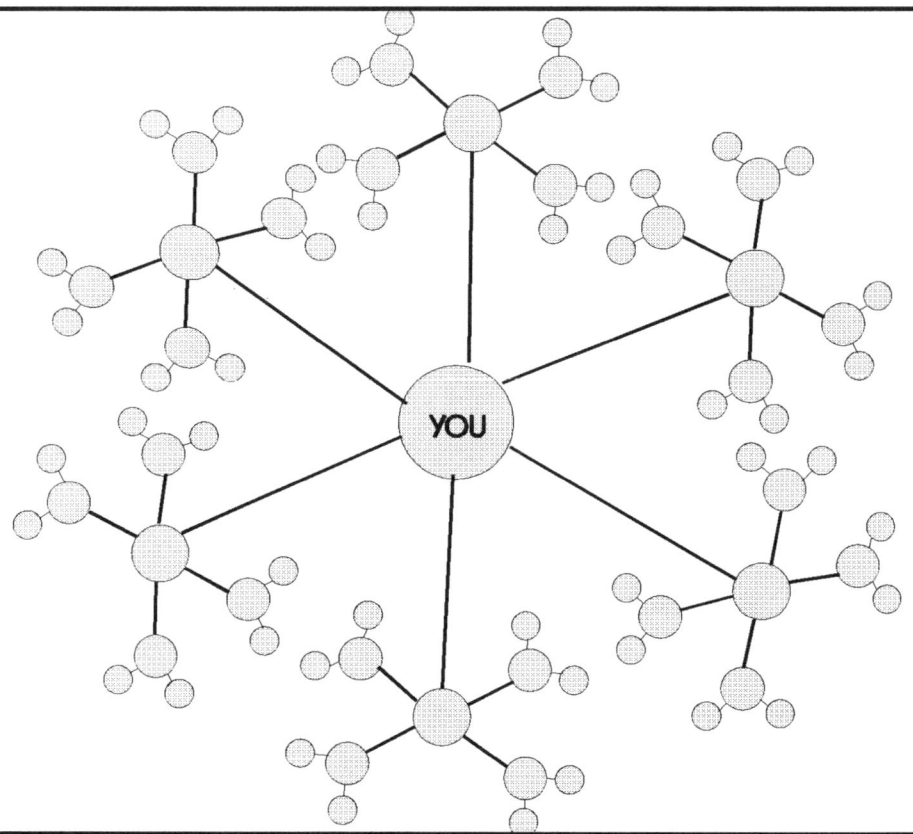

Figure 1

personally sponsored distributors in additional legs, with no depth. The real-life Silver Producer's business would look more like this (see Figure 2, next page).

Your monthly income would be approximately $1326.00 after paying out bonuses to your personally sponsored distributors, and before expenses.

Once you have qualified at that level for six months out of the fiscal year, you become a qualified Direct Distributor. Your bonus level stays at 25% of your group's total volume. You also separate from your sponsor, in that your sponsor (if also a qualified Direct Distributor) receives 4% of your group's volume instead of 25%.[1]

What incentive does your sponsor have to help you qualify as a Direct? Not much. However, with more Direct legs, more bonuses kick in. With two Direct legs and another 2500 PV in outside volume, your sponsor will qualify as a Sapphire Direct Distributor. If he and each of his Directs maintain their qualification for 12 months, he will be a Founders Sapphire Direct Distributor. This will net him some additional bonuses, as well as some hefty one-time awards. Then, when he has three qualified Direct legs, he'll be an Emerald Direct Distributor (Founders Emerald when he and his directs hold qualification for all twelve months), and eligible for more bonuses and one-time awards from Amway. At six qualified Directs, he becomes a Diamond.

Amway only pays bonuses based on the level you're actually at. So if you qualified as a Direct Distributor last year, but your volume has slipped this year, you'll be paid a Performance Bonus of 21%, or 18%, or whatever you've actually earned. If you've qualified previously as an Emerald or a Diamond, but don't requalify, you won't receive that Emerald or Diamond bonus.

However, the motivational tools business pays you bonuses based on the highest pin level you've ever achieved, whether you still qualify at that level or not.

A More Realistic Representation of a Silver Producer

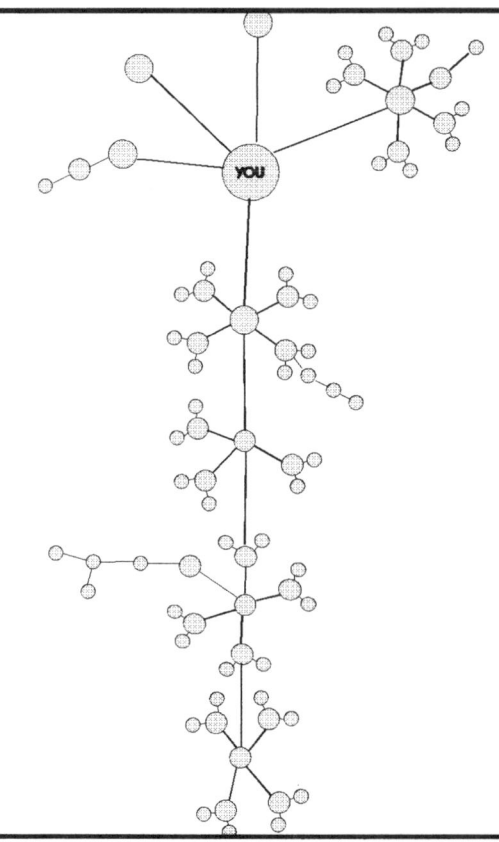

Figure 2

Tool Income and Expenses

Once your sponsor goes Direct, he receives the Amway bonuses, and he also receives his first tool bonuses. In the tool business, though, bonuses operate opposite the way they do in Amway. In Amway, as a Direct you always earn *more* on your personal group volume than anyone in your upline does. In the AMO system, as a Direct, you earn *less* on your personal group volume than anyone in your upline does. With each pin level, the percentage bonus on tools and functions increases. Jeff Probandt makes this point on his web site.[2]

For example, audio tapes comprise a large portion of system money for Emeralds and Diamonds. ICCA will duplicate audio tapes, in quantity, for $0.60 per tape. (This would include their profit.) If a tape is then sold through the organization for $6.00, that leaves $5.40 profit per tape. Here's how those profits break down: a non-direct gets no profit on tapes. A Direct Distributor sees about $0.67. An Emerald will receive about $1.83. The first Diamond gets about $2.72. The second Diamond (if any), and other pins (EDC, Double Diamond, etc.) will split the remaining $3.28. (Since this whole system is shrouded in secrecy, and I worked for a Diamond level pin, I do not have exact breakdowns on what the pin levels above Diamond receive.) There are also some variations from one leg of Yager's organization to another. Some sell the tapes for slightly less or slightly more, and the bonuses might vary. The important point to note, though, is that the greatest percentage of profit goes to the higher pin level distributor.

Another large part of the system money for Emeralds and Diamonds is the profit from functions. Emeralds and Diamonds receive bonuses every month for the tickets they sell to their own groups for Seminar & Rally. There is a scale, similar to Amway's bonus schedule for PV. Emeralds are paid anywhere from 8% to 18% of the value of tickets sold, based on the number of tickets moved through their organization. Directs receive no ticket bonus at all. The Diamond receives an additional percentage on the total tickets sold through his organization, and a promotional bonus for all tickets sold in advance.

Since, as we will show later in this chapter, the vast majority of a Diamond's income is from the system, it is worth a lot of money to him to add new Directs to his group. This often leads to situations where the Diamond, or sometimes an Emerald, actually creates a new Direct either by transferring PV into that group or actually transferring distributors from one line of sponsorship to another.

This practice was alluded to publicly for the first time in *Morrison et al v. Wilson, Amway et al*. This is a very large lawsuit, filed in Texas in January, 1998. A group of 28 Emerald-level and one Diamond Direct Distributor, are suing their upline and Amway for $200 million. Among other allegations, the Morrison suit states:

> Finally, the control of Defendants' conspiracy and evil plan to reap hundreds of millions of dollars at the expense of thousands and possibly millions of other people, got to the point that *Defendant Yager and the other Defendants conspiring among themselves and with others, would decide within the Yager organization which individual would next become an Emerald direct distributor or a Diamond level direct distributor regardless of any other individual's own achievement. They did this by manipulating the Amway point system and by transferring points from one distributor to another, realigning downline groups under a certain favored distributor and other such devices so that Defendants could maintain complete and total control over the development of Yager's downline organization.* In doing so, Defendants have destroyed the personal independent businesses of Plaintiffs. Additionally, Defendants would personally direct and coerce Plaintiffs concerning the conduct of their businesses by telling Plaintiffs which functions to attend, which upline distributors to counsel with and the specific upline distributors with whom to form associations. To do otherwise, Defendants threatened, would mean total destruction of Plaintiffs and their businesses by Defendants.[3] (Emphasis is mine.) (Morrison et al v. Amway et al)

As an Emerald, I would have a strong financial incentive to become a Diamond. My Amway income will increase some. I'll earn that extra Diamond bonus, and a one-time bonus as well. But my real income increase will come from the system.

If I am an Emerald with five, or even four qualified legs, I can create one or two more Direct legs very easily through PV transfers. At the end of the month, if I have chosen your leg to become a Direct and you haven't reached 7500 PV, I can transfer PV from my business to yours to bring you up to that magic 7500 PV number. Of course, I will lose some of my Performance Bonus from Amway. After the six-month qualifying period is over, you will transfer those points back to me. You won't be a qualified Direct any more, but that's fine with you because you'll receive tool bonus instead. And it's very fine with me, because now I've gone Diamond. I earn the Diamond Bonus from Amway, and my tool and ticket bonus is dramatically increased. The honorarium I get for speaking also increases, from around $1,000 to anywhere from $6-12,000 for a major function. Next year, I'll be able to run my own functions and make some *real* money! Even though I may not requalify as a Diamond next year – or any other year – that Amway bonus is small potatoes compared to what I'm earning from tools and tickets.

What is Wealth?

Amway distributors talk about wealth all the time. They describe their upline as "wealthy" and "very successful." Let's take a quick look at what makes a person wealthy in America.

Thomas Stanley and William Danko have been studying affluence in America, and writing about it, for twenty years. In *The Millionaire Next Door*, Stanley and Danko define wealth as "having a net worth of $1 million or more."[4] Net worth, of course, is the sum of all your assets minus all your liabilities.

What does the average millionaire look like? Images of expensive silk suits, luxury cars, and enormous homes tucked away behind gates come immediately to mind. This, however, is not the picture presented by "average" millionaires in America today. According to Stanley and Danko, the average millionaire:

- Is self-employed, in a "boring" business like welding, pest control, auctioneering, or paving
- Has an average household net worth of $3.7 million, but an annual taxable income of only $131,000
- Has an income that is less than 7% of his wealth
- Never received an inheritance
- Is well educated, with four out of five being college graduates
- Invests nearly 20% of household income each year
- Is very frugal
- Has a Visa card and a MasterCard, but not American Express Platinum card, Diners Club or Carte Blanche. Is more likely to have a Sears charge card than a card from a prestigious department store likee Neiman Marcus or Saks Fifth Avenue
- Has a clearly defined budget

- Does not live in an "upscale" neighborhood
- Does not drive a luxury or late-model car, and owns rather than leases, and
- Does not have a high-consumption lifestyle.[5] (Stanley and Danko, 8-11)

Nowhere in *The Millionaire Next Door* do Stanley and Danko mention multilevel marketing or Amway. Why? Because that's not where millionaires come from. They estimate that by the year 2005, there will be about 5.6 million millionaire households in the United States. As of this writing, fewer than 800 North American distributors have ever qualified – even once – at the Diamond level. So even if all of them are millionaires – and they're not! – the oft-repeated claim that "more millionaires come out of Amway than any other business" is nonsense.

'But wait a minute,' you say. 'My upline Diamond is wealthy! Why, he has a 7,500 square foot home on the lake, he owns four luxury cars, he has this incredible boat, his wife wears a huge diamond solitaire. He tells us how great it is to be financially free, how we need to get out of debt. They go out to eat all the time at the best restaurants, of course he's wealthy.' Unfortunately, cash flow, consumption, and wealth are not the same thing. And while the messages preached from AMO stages and tapes tell you to get out of debt, establish a savings account, and other sensible money-management tactics, the ongoing talk and continuous emphasis on display and consumption overwhelm such common sense.

We will use one Diamond as a case study. We do this simply as an example of how the money really works in the AMO system, and the flagrant lies and deceptions that are practiced to entice new prospects and delude current distributors into staying with a system that does not deliver what it promises.

One Diamond: A Case Study

This Diamond couple in the Yager AMO shows all the trappings of wealth. He wears expensive, hand-tailored suits. His shoes and boots are of the finest quality leather, eel, or other exotic skins. A large diamond glitters on his finger, gold chains dangle around his neck, and the Rolex watch is large and studded with diamonds. Her dresses flaunt well-known designer labels, and an enormous diamond graces her left hand. Quality gold and gem-studded earrings, bracelets, and necklaces vie for attention. He drives around in a luxury sports car worth well over $100,000.00. Her car, a full-size Mercedes sedan, is a bit more conservative. Several sport utility vehicles, with every available luxury option, round out the fleet.

One of their homes includes over 10,000 square feet of living space, on more than an acre in an exclusive gated community. Another home is slightly smaller, but on a desirable piece of waterfront property. Here they keep a fast boat, outfitted with all the gadgets and toys, as well as jet skis and other waterborne toys. They have a condo in a distant part of the country. After their children married, they gave each of them a substantial amount to use as a down payment on the purchase of a home.

They eat most of their meals in restaurants.

When they travel, they often charter a plane so they can bring business associates or family members along. They talk about buying their own airplane. They schedule several trips a year with family members: this is their "quality time" with children, siblings and parents.

Behind the scenes, they owe more than a quarter of a million dollars on about 30 credit cards; all their homes carry mortgages, second mortages, and equity loans; and they are two years behind in paying their Federal Income Taxes. They have no savings, yet their gross income is about $3 million.

They tell people they are wealthy.

In 1996, their gross income was $2,923,000.[6] Where did it all go?

Functions: Every year, this Diamond puts on two major functions: Family Reunion and Dream Night. Because of the graduated scale, with the leader increasing the cost of tickets as the function weekend gets closer, tickets range from $100-120 apiece. Other function income includes a percentage of all sales at the concession stands; $5-10 per distributor hotel room per night; and a percentage of all sales made by the non-Amway business speakers and entertainers.

From his ticket revenues, the Diamond has to rent the facility, and pay speakers and entertainers their fees and travel expenses. Normal expenses for these types of functions would include facility setup and teardown, running sound and lights, video/audio production and backstage management. Not all Diamonds pay for these services: many of them use unpaid labor by Direct Distributors and above. According to Probandt,

> [Direct Distributors] have now earned the right to come earlier to the functions and work the various positions that are required to put on a large convention. Remember, they paid their way in like everyone else but now they may, for example, drive a transportation van all weekend. This is one way the Diamonds keep the cost of these functions down and the profit up. They tell people over and over that it is an honor to serve their upline.[7] (Probandt, "The System")

Profit on functions: $1,281,000 - $997,000 = $284,000.

Speaking Fees: This is the honorarium the Diamond receives for speaking at other Diamonds' functions. $38,000.00

Ticket Bonuses: This is the bonus the Diamond receives from his upline AMO for tickets sold to his organization for monthly seminars & rallies, Free Enterprise Day, and Go Diamond Weekend. Included is a promotional bonus on tickets sold in advance. He then must pay bonus out to the Emeralds who qualify for ticket bonus.

Neither the ticket bonus income nor expense are truly representative of the money flowing into this organization from ticket sales. The financial arrangements in the AMO system are, of course, extremely complicated. This makes it very difficult to analyze the information. In this particular Diamond organization, monthly Seminars & Rallies are run by an AMO which is farther upline. Some of the Directs, Sapphires and Emeralds buy their tickets and receive their ticket bonuses from the Diamond in this case study; others buy their tickets and receive their bonuses from the upline AMO organization.

Profit on Ticket Bonus: $167,000 - $82,000 = $85,000.

Sales of Tools: This includes a few tapes or videos produced by the Diamond from his own functions, a monthly newsletter for his AMO, and some sales aids, and sales of books which he purchased directly from the publisher or book distributor and resold, instead of ordering from his upline. It does **not** include any tools sold directly by InterNET Services Corp. or by his upline Diamond to distributors in his organization.

Expense includes the cost of producing the tapes and videos, and the wholesale cost of the books purchased from the publishers.

Profit on Tool Sales: $282,000 - $266,000 = $16,000.

Tool Bonuses: This is the bonus he receives on all of the tapes, books, videos, and non-Amway produced sales aids sold to distributors in his organization.

Diamond Income and Expenses			
	Income	Expenses	Profit
Functions[1]	$ 1,281,000	$ 997,000	$284,000
Tool Bonuses	909,000	681,000	228,000
Tool Sales/Expenses[2]	282,000	266,000	16,000
Ticket Bonuses	167,000	82,000	85,000
Product Bonuses	130,000	34,000	96,000
Product Sales to Distributors/ Expenses	78,000	113,000	(35,000)
International	14,000	18,000	(4,000)
Shipping[3]	6,000	23,000	(17,000)
Speaking Fees	38,00		38,000
Charity[4]		12,000	(12,000)
Misc. Income	18,000		18,000
Travel[5]		123,000	(123,000)
Meals		7,000	(7,000)
Auto[6]		50,000	(50,000)
Interest[7]		27,000	(27,000)
Telephone and Amvox		45,000	(45,0006)
Salaries for Office Staff		80,000	(80,000)

Table 7

Profit on Tool Bonus: $909,000 - $681,000 = $228,000.

Product Sales to Distributors:[8] Because of the way Amway's distribution system works, most Direct Distributors receive products for themselves and their personal group directly from Amway. This figure represents only those products that were sold directly by this Diamond to distributors in his personal group. This does not represent his organization's overall purchases from Amway.

Diamond Income and Expenses			
Office Expenses, including			
Office Mortgage		13,000.00	(13,000.00)
Leased Equipment		2,000	(2,000)
Sales Tax		3,0004	(3,000)
Insurance		2,000	(2,000)
Accounting Fees		2,000	(2,000)
Utilities		5,000	(5,0000)
Office Equipment		6,000	(6,000)
Misc.		4,172.46	(4,172.46)
TOTAL[8]	$2,923,000	2,600,000	323,000

Table 8

Table Notes

1. Function expenses include fees paid to speakers.
2. Sales of tools referred to here do *not* include tools sold directly by InterNET Services Corp. or by this Diamond's upline Diamond to distributors in his organization.
3. Includes UPS, mail, postage meter.
4. Much of this amount was collected at the Sunday morning service at major functions. Very little – if any – was the Diamond's own contribution.
5. Includes airfare, hotels, rental condo, auto rental, air charters, meals.
6. Interest includes credit card, loan, line of credit interest and servicing charges. It does not include mortgage interest.
7. Includes fuel, insurance, leasing costs, service.
8. This total does **not** include cash collected but not declared from Introductory Seminar admissions and from cash sales of tools and tickets at functions.

This figure is larger than the income from product sales, reflecting products withdrawn for personal use, products used to stock the office, and products sold to distributors and not paid for or (rarely) given away as samples.

Profit (Loss) on Products: $78,000 - $113,000= ($35,000).

Product Bonuses: Income from Amway. This includes Performance Bonus, Profit Sharing, and Pearl and Emerald bonus. In this particular year, there was no Diamond bonus as he was only a qualified Emerald. Out of this he must in turn pay out bonuses to non-Direct, personally sponsored distributors. As a Profit Sharing Direct Distributor, a few thousand dollars of the Profit Sharing Bonus he receives from Amway is in the form of mutual funds. Of the nearly $3 million in income, this is the only portion that comes from the Sales & Marketing Plan, and wouldn't sustain his lifestyle for more than a month or two.

Profit on Product Bonuses: $130,000 - $34,000= $96,000

International: This represents the "processing fees" charged to distributors in the organization for handling the referral of prospects in international markets. There are some costs he incurred for international business, so this category shows a small loss.

Profit (Loss) on International: $14,000 - $18,000 = ($4,000).

Shipping: The reimbursement received from distributors for the cost of shipping their products and tools to them is shown as income. Expense includes shipping to distributors, which was reimbursed, as well as postage and shipping costs incurred as normal overhead.

Profit (Loss) on Shipping: $6,000 - $23,000= ($17,000).

Miscellaneous: $18,000

Note that these income figures do not include some items. Standard proecedure for this Diamond has been to collect cash for admission to Introductory Seminars, pay the room rental with that cash, and pocket the rest. Admission to Leadership Meetings at major functions is handled the same way. Some of the cash collected for sales of tools at functions does not find its way into any bank account or accountant's ledger either. These numbers can be significant. If only 1,000 distributors at each major function attend the leadership meeting, and pay $5.00 at the door, that's $10,000 per year. Each Introductory Seminar generates several hundred dollars in cash. Tool sales at functions can easily run into six figures.

Only 4.447% of this Diamond's declared total gross income actually comes from Amway Corp. He owns no other businesses or investments which would produce income for him.

The remaining categories are all overhead expenses: travel, auto, office expenses, and the like, totaling $374,000. As with other financial aspects of an AMO business, though, the flow of money is intentionally very complicated and difficult to analyze. For example, the category of "Travel" often includes fares, hotel rooms, and meals for family members who are traveling with the Diamonds, but have no legitimate business purpose for being there. The same is true for dining out. Telephone and Amvox charges are paid from the business accounts and used as business deductions. Credit cards are used indiscrimately for a combination of business and personal purchases. While it may be obvious that there is no business deduction for a $600 bathing suit, an $800 pair of earrings, or a $300 pair of Italian loafers, the interest on that purchase may be charged off as a business expense.

Not shown here is the outstanding debt to the IRS. In 1997, this Diamond had still not paid all of his taxes (including penalties and interest) for 1995, nor had he paid anything for 1996 or estimated payments for 1997. This means that the taxpayers have for several years been subsidizing the illusion of wealth he presents – his travel, his homes, luxury cars, and other expensive habits.

There is nothing on his tax returns to indicate that he is an Amway distributor. His profession is listed as "Marketer," and his wife is a "Homemaker." Other items metamorphose into something else by the time the tax returns are filed. Function tickets, for example, become "Merchandise." This is done to give the impression that their "marketing" business is not an MLM.

On paper, this Diamond shows a net income of $323,000, or a little more than 10% of his gross income, and just slightly more than his credit card debt. Guidelines in *The Millionaire Next Door* would suggest he should have a net worth of about $1.6 million to be considered wealthy. The reality is, even with the small amount of equity he has in his homes, his net worth is probably not even 10% of that figure.

This Diamond creates the illusion that he lives on the financial peaks, but closer examination shows that he's really down in the basement. While he does, indeed, have a very large cash flow, his assets are negligible and his liabilities enormous. He is anything but wealthy.

What's Wrong with this Picture?

Why is this a problem? Many business owners – in fact, a great many Americans in all walks of life – live beyond their means, and try to show more material success than they actually have. Indebtedness has become one of the hallmarks of contemporary society. Why pick on the Diamonds?

Core distributors frequently comment that they don't care whether their upline profits on tools. 'The tools are reasonably priced,' they trumpet, 'and because I've listened to these tapes and read these books and attended these functions, I'm a better person. So if my upline makes a little on them, that's fine with me.' I occasionally hear stories from distributors who claim that the tools in the Amway business helped them advance in their regular jobs.

When I owned another business, before Amway, I actively searched for tapes and books on goal setting and positive thinking, and attended seminars and workshops, because they helped me develop my business. What is the difference between those materials and the tools I purchased from my AMO upline?

None of the authors, speakers, or retailers I bought tapes and books from outside of the AMO pretended that they were supplying these items out of "love," or because they "cared" about my success. They had a product I wanted, and I paid a fair price to purchase it.

However, when you get started in the Amway business, you are instructed in the strongest possible terms to trust your upline. After all, he has your best interests at heart, and because of his vested interest in your success will never tell you to do anything that will hurt your business! This instruction is reinforced at every Introductory Seminar and Seminar & Rally you attend, where your upline is edified and you are told again and again how loving, caring, unselfish and trustworthy he is. You are taught to demand the same level of trust from those you sponsor.

As a consumer, you know when you buy a new TV set, a car, a music CD or book through normal retail channels that somebody is making a profit from your purchase. If you are a college student, and the required textbook is written by your professor, you can be reasonably certain that he's earning something from your textbook purchase. If you are bold enough, or cynical enough, to question your upline about the profits made from AMO tools, you will hear responses like this: 'Well, Ruth, you know your upline Direct invests a lot of money in keeping an inventory of tapes and books on hand for the distributors. Dexter (or Bill, or Jack) has set it up so that he gets a little break on the price of those tools, just to help him offset the money he has tied up in inventory.' Or he will misdirect you: 'Sure there's money in the tapes! That's only fair, isn't it? Each speaker gets a few cents on each tape of one of his speeches that's sold. It's a speaking royalty. You don't have a problem with that, do you?' One Direct, who challenged his Diamond as to why he hadn't been fully informed about the tool bonuses, was told, 'you didn't ask the right questions,' as though somehow the lack of disclosure was the distributor's responsibility.

As an Amway distributor, your relationship with your sponsor, upline Direct Distributor, or Diamond is *not* an "arm's length transaction." Your upline showed you a marketing plan, and assured you that it represents incomes that are achievable from selling Amway products and sponsoring others to do the same. He showed you books and videos depicting massive amounts of wealth, which were represented as the reward for building a successful Amway distributorship.[**] He has promised that you, too, can own homes, cars, boats, furs, jewels, like those you see the Diamonds flaunting if you trust the people in your upline and do what they tell you to do for two to five years. He has assured you that your upline will do nothing that will hurt you. You must trust them, and rely on their wisdom and advice.

Would you be so quick to sign up as a distributor if he had told you clearly, 'look, the real income here is not from moving Amway products and services, it's from getting people hooked on motivational tapes and functions. Less than 5% of my income really comes from Amway, the rest is from the system. But I'll tell you what. If you'll recruit people using this Amway vehicle, and if you'll set the example by consuming a minimum of $5,000.00 worth of books, tapes and functions per year and get 600 other people in six different legs to do the same thing and use some Amway products too, you'll be a Diamond. Then you, too, can run millions of dollars a year through your business. Oh, and these houses you see, this boat, this airplane, this fur coat my wife is wearing, the jewelry... the bank and credit card companies own most of it. But you'll need these things to

---

[**] Using the *Profiles of Success* or other **lifestyle** materials as sponsoring tools violates Amway's rules. But, like so many others, this rule is not enforced.

make other people think you're successful, and then it'll be easier for you to recruit people....'? Would you sign up for the Standing Order Tape program, or the Book Of the Month or Video Of the Month? Would you attend every Introductory Seminar, Seminar & Rally and major function? When your upline tells you, 'look, you really need this particular tape, it's going to help you jump-start your business,' would you trust his recommendation and buy it without hesitation? Or would you consider his profit motive for selling you that tape, and decide on a *businesslike* basis whether you need it and it fits into your business budget?

Many AMO leaders insist that the tapes, books and functions truly are necessary if a distributor is to develop a successful business. 'The issue here isn't the money for the tools,' they assert, 'the tools help you grow and develop succes habits and successful ways of thinking. Without them you can't succeed.'

If the issue is not the money, then why don't they sell the tapes for the sixty cents it costs to produce them?[9] Since the Diamonds can purchase books directly from the publisher at 50% off retail, why not sell them for that price? But they don't. They sell the books at a 100% markup, and the tapes at a markup of over 1,000%. (Yes, you read that number right – one thousand percent.) Videos are marked up about 500%, and CD's about 200-300%.

I believe it is critical for Amway distributors, recruits, and prospects to understand where the money comes from in an AMO because of the relationship of trust distributors demand of those they sponsor. As long as the truth is kept hidden from the majority of distributors, the upline/downline relationship will breed abuses.

AMO leaders have always tried to keep their real source of income – sales of motivation – a secret from their distributors. This has led to other secrets, and other deceptions. It has led the AMOs to create well-planned programs of manipulation to keep distributors plugged in to the system. It is why the American Family foundation, FACTNet, and other cultic study groups list Amway as an organization with cultlike characteristics. According to Rick Ross, cult exit counselor, "Some of [Amway's] persuasion techniques seem to utilize aspects of 'thought reform'... Also, based upon email I have received and complaints – the mindset of the organization members is at times is 'cult'-like."[10] It is why many former distributors belive that the AMOs are indeed cults.

NINE: What Is a Cult?

When you meet the friendliest people you have ever known, who introduce you to the most loving group of people you've ever encountered, and you find the leader to be the most inspired, caring, compassionate and understanding person you've ever met, and then you learn that the cause of the group is something you never dared hope could be accomplished, and all of this sounds too good to be true, it probably is too good to be true! Don't give up your education, your hopes and ambitions, to follow a rainbow.[1]

We all know what cults are, don't we? A cult is that group of crazed religious fanatics in the Guyana jungles who committed mass murder and suicide. A cult is the group of militants who took on the FBI in Waco, TX. Or a cult is that group of strange androgynes in San Diego who drank poison when the looked-for spaceship didn't follow the Hale-Bopp comet and pick them up.

These are extreme and frightening examples of cults, but unfortunately cults can wear very ordinary faces.

Amway is very concerned about accusations of cultism, which are widespread enough that they have posted a page on their website at www.amway.com denying that the Amway business is a cult. Unfortunately, the word *cult* has many implications, carries strong emotional overtones, and is greatly misunderstood. We will take a brief look at what a cult is, and how cultic relationships and organizations differ from their non-cultic counterparts. After this general overview, we will take an objective look at Amway and the AMOs to see whether they meet any of those criteria. At the outset we will point out that neither Amway nor the AMOs have ever shown the extremes of behavior in the examples above. In taking a broad look at what sets a cult apart from a non-cultic organization, not every item will apply to every cult. A cult *will* include the majority of items.

Steven Hassan has become one of the foremost cult-exit counselors in the United States today, and the author of a definitive book on the mind-control tactics of cults. In *Combatting Cult Mind Control,* Hassan presents a chilling picture of the cult phonemenon in America:

> In the past twenty years, the destructive cult phenomenon has mushroomed into a problem of tremendous social and political importance. It is estimated that there are now approximately three thousand destructive cults in the United States, involving as many as three million people. They come in many different types and sizes... Some, however, are clearly more dangerous than others. Not content to exercise their power simply over the lives of their members, they have an agenda to gain political power and use it to reshape American society – and in the case of some of them, even the world.

> Considering how well destructive cults have been able to shield themselves from public scrutiny in the past few years, it might seem alarmist to regard them as a threat to individual liberty and society as a whole. Yet, they are influencing the political landscape by extensive lobbying efforts and electioneering for candidates...

> Since all destructive cults believe that the ends justify the means, they ... violate, in the most profound and fundamental way, the civil liberties of the people they recruit.... A destructive cult distinguishes itself from a normal social or religious group by subjecting its members to deception or other damaging influences to keep them in the group.[2] (Hassan, 36-7)

Hassan describes four types of cults: Religious, Political, Psychotherapy/educational, and Commercial. We are concerned here with the Commercial Cult.

> **Commercial cults** believe in the dogma of greed. They deceive and manipulate people to work for little or no pay in the hope of getting rich. There are many pyramid-style or multi-level marketing organizations that promise big money but fleece their victims. They then destroy their victims' self-esteem so that they will not complain.[3] (Hassan, 40)

Robert Jay Lifton has been studying mind-control practices since the 1950's. He describes cults as "a cluster of groups with certain characteristics."[4] These characteristics include:

- charismatic leadership
- use of "coercive persuasion" or "thought reform"
- a "pattern of manipulation and exploitation from above [by leaders]... and idealism from below [by recruits]."[5] (Lifton, xii)

Margaret Thaler Singer is a clinical psychologist and emeritus adjunct professor of the Department of Psychology, University of California, Berkeley, and has been studying cults for fifty years. She has counseled and interviewed over 3,000 current and former cult members, and written numerous books and articles on the subject. Singer states:

> Currently, depending on how one defines a cult, there are anywhere from three thousand to five thousand cults in the United States alone. Over the past two decades as many as twenty million people have been involved for varying periods of time in one or another of these groups... In the 1980s and 1990s, we have seen cults seduce people of all ages and all income brackets... today's cultic groups have so professionalized their approaches and techniques of persuasion that they are moving well beyond the fringe and into the mainstream. They want you.[6] (Singer, 5-6)

The Cultic Relationship

According to Singer, it is possible to determine whether a relationship is cultic. Begin to question:

- the origin of the group and the role of the leader
- the power structure, or relationship between the leader(s) and followers
- do they use a coordinated program of persuasion[7] (Singer, 7)
- do they consistently use deception during the recruiting process[8] (Hassan, 99)

1. First, look at the group itself and the leader.

   Determine the origin of the group. Was the organization formed by a group of like-minded people who got together to carry out a mutually agreed-upon purpose? Or did the leader create the group, gathering followers who were obedient to him? In a non-cultic relationship, the leader is elected or appointed by the members. In a cult, the leader is self-appointed. Who is the leader? What is his background? Does he live in affluence while the members of the group live in relative poverty?

2. **Notice the power structure, or relationship between the leader (or leaders) and the followers**

Examine the lines of communication in the group. Is there consistent, *two-way* communication between the leader and the members? Does the leader make suggestions to members which they are free to either respond to or ignore? Does the communication come from the top down? Is the leader willing to listen to suggestions, complaints, or problems that members have with the group? Are members expected to do what they're told by the leader? Are they punished if they do not follow the leader's orders? Does the leader make life decisions for the members? Does he control their time or their environment?

In a non-cultic relationship, members are free to decide whether the leader's advice is reasonable and appropriate, and to act accordingly. In a cultic relationship, members do not have this freedom. If they complain or make suggestions, they are told that the group is correct, and the complainer is "defective." If they disregard the leader's advice, they will be punished. The punishment can be very direct – physical or sexual abuse, for example, as found in the Jonestown community – or indirect, with emotional and psychological manipulation of the member by the leader.

Watch out if the group leader routinely controls members, or induces them to follow his "advice" by threats (expressed or implied) or manipulation of guilt or fear, on such things as:
* where they live
* the food they eat
* the purchases they make
* whether or not they seek medical treatment
* how they raise their children

- their relationship with their spouse
- their relationship with other family members or with friends who are not members of the group
- and the activities they engage in during non-working hours.

Such life controls indicate a cultic relationship.

3. **Become sensitive to the use of a coordinated program of persuasion**

In a non-cultic relationship, members of civic organizations, churches, and other volunteer groups you might want to join, are free to weigh the leader's suggestions and determine for themselves an appropriate course of action. In a cultic relationship, members are subject to deceptive mind-control practices (guilt, for example) which render their judgment unreliable and make *freedom of choice* difficult or impossible. This is a huge subject, which we will come back to.

4. **Do you notice consistent use of deception during the recruitment process?**

Does the group actively recruit members, or do most recruits approach the group and request membership? Are the real goals of the group the same goals that were presented at the start of the recruitment process? Does the group give new recruits access to information about the group in small steps, or is all information available to the new recruit? What about the name of the group? Have you heard of this group before? Does the stated group name change during the recruitment process?

If a group is examined in light of these factors, it will quickly become obvious whether the group tends to be cultic.

Other analysts remark on these same characteristics, with different wording.

Deceptive Mind Control

Steve Hassan was recruited into the Moonies while an idealistic young college student. He quickly rose to a high level of responsibility in the organization, and knew Sun Myung Moon personally. Why, then, did he leave the Moonies?

I left the group because I came to see objectively what I had been doing. I had devoted myself to a 'fantasy' created in the Moonie indoctrination workshops. I thought I was following the Messiah, the person who would be able to end war, poverty, disease, and corruption, and establish a Kingdom of Heaven on Earth. I didn't mind sacrificing myself for these noble causes. I thought that as a member, I was teaching people the ultimate standard of love and truth, and living an exemplary life.

Instead, I realized to my horror that I had learned to compromise my integrity in the name of God. I realized that the higher I rose in the organization, and the closer I got to Moon, the more obsessed I had become. Power became almost an addiction, and I began making choices based on what would protect and enhance my power, not on what was morally right.

I left when I realized that deception and mind control can never be part of any legitimate spiritual movement: that through their use, the group had created a virtual 'Hell on Earth,' a kingdom of slaves. Once I was able to realize that even though I *wanted* to believe it was true (Moon as Messiah, Divine Principle as Truth), *my belief didn't make it true.* I saw that even if I remained in the group for another fifty years, the fantasy I was sacrificing myself for would never come true.

By being given some clear definitions of mind control, I was able to see clearly how I had been victimized and how I had learned to victimize others. I personally had to come to terms with my own values, beliefs, and ideals. Once I did that, even though I had invested so much of myself in the group, become a leader, and developed close bonds with many members, I had to walk away. I could never go back to becoming a 'true believer' again.[9] (Hassan, p. 167)

One of the keys to a successful mind-control relationship is that the *subject must be kept unaware that he is being manipulated.* This is where the image of locked rooms and rubber truncheons in relation to mind control comes apart. Someone who is being obviously victimized – held prisoner, beaten, tortured – is much more resistant to mind-control or thought reform than is the person who is being manipulated with words and friendly faces. Singer credits author George Orwell, author of *1984* and *Animal Farm*, with being the first to recognize that *language* is the key to mental manipulation, not force: the smiling Big Brother is more potent than the jack-booted soldier.

Singer describes six conditions of a cultic relationship: the stronger these conditions are, the more effective the mind-control program will be.[10] (Singer, 64)

1. Keep the person unaware that there is an agenda to control or change the person. The recruit is forced to adapt in a series of steps which are so small that he is not aware of the program's true goals.

2. Control the person's social and/or physical environment; especially control the person's time.

3. Systematically create a sense of powerlessness in the person. This is done by *stripping you of your support system and your ability to act independently.* Once you've been separated from your friends and relatives, you lose confidence in your own perceptions. If you're overly tired, this confidence-losing process can be speeded up.

4. Manipulate a system of rewards, punishments, and experiences in such a way as to inhibit behavior that reflects the person's former social identity. Old beliefs and old patterns of behavior are defined as irrelevant.

5. Manipulate a system of rewards, punishments, and experiences in order to promote learning of the group's ideology or belief system and group-approved behaviors. *The more complicated and filled with contradictions the new system is and the more difficult it is to learn, the more effective the conversion process will be.*

6. Put forth a closed system of logic and an authoritarian structure that permits no feedback and refuses to be modified except by leadership approval or executive order. *If you criticize or complain, the leader or peers allege that you are defective, not the organization.... In cultic groups, the individual member is always wrong and the system is always right.*[11] (Singer, 64-67)

Follow another analysis of cultism: Robert Lifton's eight psychological themes. Cults invoke these to promote changes in members' attitudes and behavior. Summarized, these include:

1. Control over the environment and communication in the group.

2. Use of jargon exclusive to the group. This sets members apart from the rest of society, since only other members can understand you. It identifies you as "one of us."

3. An "us-versus-them" orientation, with "us" representing what is pure and "them" representing what is impure. Since all impurities originate with "them," an individual member can easily be shamed and humiliated.

4. Confession, used to make the member feel close to the group and estranged from nonmembers.

5. Manipulation of members to make them think their new feelings and behavior have arisen spontaneously instead of being carefully programmed.

6. Teaching members to ignore their own experiences. and interpret reality based on what the group "believes."

7. A patina of science (or pseudo-science) over the leader's teaching to foster credibility.

8. Emphasizing that members are an "elite" or "select" group, creating a further gulf between "us" and "them."[12] (Groenveld, internet)

Who Joins Cults?

A group does not have to be religious to be cultic in behavior. High demand groups can be commerical, political and psychological. Be aware, especially if you are a bright, intelligent and idealistic person. The most likely person to be caught up in this type of behavioural system is the one who says "I won't get caught. It will never happen to me. I am too intelligent for that sort of thing."[13] (Groenveld, internet)

On the surface, it might seem completely farfetched to look for cultlike characteristics in a *business*. But according to Singer, today's fastest-growing cults are "those centered around New Age thinking and certain personal improvement training, ... or prosperity programs. These latter cults are most likely to be the kind you or your friends may have come across or been influenced by, perhaps even seduced by, for a period of time."[14] (Singer. 13)

Nobody is immune to the lure of the cult. We like to feel that we are invulnerable to cult deception, but

> Research indicates that approximately two-thirds of those who have joined cults came from normal, functioning families. ... Of the remaining third, only about 5 to 6 percent had major psychological difficulties prior to joining a cult.[15] (Singer, 17)

Hassan points out:

> Often people look at a cult victim and say mistakenly, "What a weak-minded person; he must have been looking for a way to escape responsibility and have someone control his life." In that way people deny the reality that the same thing could happen to them.... Our need to believe that we are invulnerable, though, is actually a weakness that can easily be played upon by cult recruiters.[16] (Hassan, 43-44)

Cults today are extremely sophisticated in their programs of deception.

> In most instances today, there is nothing casual in the way these sophisticated techniques are employed, nor is there anything mysterious in the way they achieve their most predictable and profound effects. Like the distracting watch fob of the mesmerist, the well-known physical stresses used by cult and group leaders serve only to weaken people to suggestion and command.... They are controlled by the specific ideas, beliefs, opinions, emotions, suggestions and direct orders people receive from cult recruiters, sect leaders, self-help trainers, pop therapists, born-again preachers and others, in personal conversations and group rituals delivered amid the atmospheres of warmth, love and total acceptance.[17] (Conway and Siegelman, 92-3)

Let's take a look at how mind control works in the next chapter.

TEN: How Does Mind Control Work?

Deceptive mind-control is an ongoing process, not a single incident. It ultimately makes the person dependent on the organization. "There are no secret drugs or potions. It is just words and group pressures, put together in packaged forms."[1] (Singer, 57)

> ... this attack is carried out under a variety of guises and conditions – and rarely does it include forced confinement or direct physical coercion. Rather, it is a subtle and powerful psychological process of destabilization and induced dependency.[2] (Singer, 60)

Destabilization and *induced dependency* occur when a person is removed from sources of "real world" feedback. When normal relationships with family and friends are disrupted or ended; when the person stops reading the newspaper, watching news programming, or getting news and viewpoints from sources outside the cult, the person becomes dependent on the cult for all of his information. Leaders then can filter information to the person through the perspective of the cult's agenda. Since the person is also allowing leaders to make life decisions for him, and since leaders are adept at *reframing* or interpreting the person's life's events according to their agenda instead of his own experience, the person quickly loses confidence in himself and becomes dependent on the cult and its leadership.

Following are brief descriptions of the most common techniques generally used by cultic organizations. In Chapter Eleven, we will look specifically at the AMOs in light of what we've learned about cults and cultic relationships.

Physiological Techniques

The physiological techniques are used to actually change the way the member is functioning physically in ways that will make him more suggestible or malleable to the leader's purposes. Very often, when the member experiences these changes, the leader will reframe, or reinterpret, the member's experience in light of what the leader's goals are. Moral or spiritual significance may be attributed to normal physical symptoms.

Hyperventilation. Hyperventilation is caused by overbreathing. This condition can be induced intentionally, as when breathing techniques of many Eastern religions are abused, or without the members' awareness through loud shouting, chanting and singing. Mild hyperventilation can cause dizziness or light-headedness, feelings of being "high," and will diminish critical thought and judgment. Prolonged or vigorous hyperventilaion causes more severe distress, including numbness and tingling at the extremities, feelings of fear or panic, ringing in the ears, pounding of the heart, or even muscle cramps and convulsions. Fainting often occurs as the result of moderate to heavy hyperventilation.

Repetitive Motion. Repetitive motion can include clapping, swaying, spinning, and some types of dancing. Almost any repetitive motion can help to alter the person's awareness. When clapping or swaying is combined with chanting or singing, the effects of hyperventilation are combined with repetitive motion.

Sleep Deprivation. Everyone experiences a lack of sleep from time to time. Staying up to care for a sick child, "pulling an all-nighter" to get the term paper or work-related project finished, driving through the night to reach a vacation destination sooner are all temporary interruptions to our normal sleep cycles. After a night or even two of inadequate sleep, the healthy person can quickly recover. However, cults use inadequate rest – sometimes lasting weeks or months – to weaken their members mentally and emotionally and make them more suggestible.

Change in Diet. An abrupt change in diet – even a change to a more healthful diet – can lead to initial gastro-intestinal discomfort. The dietary change will also affect the person's energy levels. Depending on the type of change, one may feel temporarily energized or "high," or may feel sluggish and lethargic.

Hormonal Changes. Poor diet, sleep deprivation and stress can lead to hormonal changes, with predictable side effects.

Psychological Techniques.

Naturalistic Trance Induction. The word *hypnosis* refers to the process of putting a person in a state of trance. The hypnosis can be either overt, as in the stereotype of the gold watch swinging back and forth and the hypnotist announcing "you are getting sleepy…" or it can be induced *without the awareness of the person.* The latter is called *naturalistic trance induction.*

Trance. While in a trance state, the individual's concentration is highly focused, and he suspends critical judgment. This makes him very amenable to suggestion. The trance state is characterized by:

+ Modification of consciousness or awareness
+ Dimming of critical-evaluative thinking
+ Passive-receptive mode of mental processing instead of an active mode
+ Lack of reflection or evaluation of what we hear or see
+ Suspension of rational analysis
+ Suspension of conscious decision making
+ Blurring of boundaries between imagination and reality
+ Blurring of boundaries between the factual and what we desire to be true.

Thought Stopping. Thought stopping techniques are used by cult members to avoid thinking "bad" or "negative" thoughts about their cult group, or to avoid thinking critically about it at all. Singing, humming, repeating a slogan, praying, or meditating will be performed mechanically, because the members have been taught that these techniques will help them be more effective, or will help them to grow. Hassan claims that "thought-stopping is the most direct way to short-circuit a person's ability to test reality."[3] (Hassan, 63) And thought stopping can induce a trance state.

Guided Imagery/Guided Fantasy. Using words to create mental images is called *guided imagery*. This can be used to induce a trance state.

Indirect Directives. These are methods used to obtain compliance without actually ordering or directing the person. The leader needs only to imply that something should be done, and if the person feels cooperative, and is vulnerable due to fatigue or stress, the person will do it.

Trickery. The trickery used by many cult leaders is the same kind of trickery used by charlatans throughout the ages. The "medium" who finds a way to go through the victim's purse to find names or photographs; the leader of the healing cult who finds devious ways to determine the health or other problems of newcomers to his "services" so that he can shout out "inspired" information directed at them are well-known examples of this type of trickery. The AMO leader needs to know your dreams, thoughts and concerns. Usually, just by showing interest in you, he'll get you to open up and "share" the information he needs to manipulate you.

Revision/Rewriting of Personal History. This is important to the cult leaders for several reasons. Normally, the cult draws a strong line between "us" and "them," with the cult comprising the elite. Stories by cult members of past histories which show how bad the world "outside" is compared to the wonderful world inside the cult are powerful persuaders for newcomers. Cult members learn from listening to older members' stories how to revise their own histories in acceptable ways.

Peer Pressure. People naturally want to fit in with their present social grouping. When moving in a new social environment, a person will model his behavior on the behavior of those around him. Therefore, the cult will train its members in the "right" way to behave to serve as strong behavior models for newer members or recruits. Peer pressure is also a strong force in shaping the behavior of old members.

Emotional Manipulation. Emotional manipulation typically includes the manipulation of fear, guilt, and shame to make the member dependent on the cult. In many cults, strong phobias are induced to make the member believe that he cannot survive outside the safety of the cult.

Behavior/Environment Control

By controlling a member's environment (what food he eats, how much sleep he gets, where he lives or works, the clothing he wears, his material resources, and how he spends his time), the cult can ultimately control his mind. *Belief will follow behavior.* Why is this? If you change a person's behavior, his thoughts and beliefs will change in an attempt to reduce the internal conflict, or dissonance. This is called *cognitive dissonance.*

Information Control

In many totalistic cults, people have minimal access to non-cult newspapers, magazines, TV and radio. This is partly because they are kept so busy they don't have free time. When they do read, it is primarily cult-generated propaganda or material that has been censored to 'help' members stay focused.

Information control also extends across all relationships. People are not allowed to talk to each other about anything critical of the leader, doctrine, or organization.... Most importantly, people are told to avoid contact with ex-members or critics.... Information is usually compartmentalized to keep members from knowing the big picture.... Cult members naturally feel they know more about what's going on in their group than outsiders do, but in counseling ex-members I find that they often know the least.[4] (Hassan, 65)

The combined effect of a sophisticated package which includes the elements of physiological and psychological mind-control techniques, behavior/environment control, and information control can be devastating.

These ritualized communication practices are as powerful as any physical force in their potential to disrupt and impair the brain's information-processing activities. By tampering with basic distinctions between reality and fantasy... or simply by stilling the workings of the mind over time, these intense communication practices may break down vital faculties of mind. *There is also growing evidence that they may organically impair crucial working connections in the brain's underlying synaptic networks and neurochemical channels and, in their extremes, physically destroy long-standing information-processing pathways in the brain.*[5] *(Conway and Siegelman, 149-50)*

This means the deceptive mind-control practices of the cult can produce – and in many cases have produced – irreversible changes in a person's ability to function in the "real" world.

ELEVEN: Is Amway A Cult?

The Coliseum is dark, except for the spotlight on the stage. Doug Wead, an Amway Diamond, is speaking. Doug is a favorite speaker on Yager stages during the middle 1980's. A Baptist minister by background, Doug exhibits a wide streak of irreverence about "the business".

"Some of you have heard that this business is a cult. I wish it was a cult," Wead announces plaintively. "In a cult, everyone does what you tell them to do. I can't get my people to do nothin'!"

The coliseum erupts with clapping, whistling, and laughter from the audience. That's true, anybody says this is a cult obviously doesn't know what they're talking about. I can't get my people to do nothin' either! Distributors nudge one another and laugh.

Amway Corporation categorically denies accusations of cultism. Their World Wide Web site claims:

Why do Amway meetings appear to some people like a cult? Amway meetings are full of energy, enthusiasm, and excitement – just like most sales motivation meetings – because this is a proven way to motivate people to sell.... This enthusiasm motivates our distributors to help and support one another, and that builds sales.... That is one big reason why Amway distributors are so optimistic and upbeat.[1] (Amway Corp., internet)

I've been involved in sales for many years, and am very familiar with "enthusiastic meetings." This by itself would not raise accusations of cultism, which distributors deny more hotly than Amway does. "Anyone who suggests that Amway is a cult just doesn't understand our special business. After all, we're not mindless robots, rotely following our leader's orders," the thinking goes. Are we?

Sadly, members of many cults feel the same way, hotly denying that their "special" group is a cult. AMO leaders sometimes joke about it, telling distributors that they *need* a good brainwashing to clear their minds of all the "negative junk" that's built up over the years. Compare Hassan's similar reaction.

> When I was in the Moonies, I knew I hadn't been brainwashed. I do remember, however, Moon giving us a speech in which he said a popular magazine had accused him of brainwashing us. He declared, 'Americans' minds are very dirty – full of selfish materialism and drugs – and they need a heavenly brainwashing!' We all laughed.[2] (Hassan, 56)

Cults Recruit Deceptively. Do the AMOs?

> The basic feature of most cult *recruitment* is *deception....* [Cults] operate under the assumption that people are too "ignorant"... to recognize what is best for them. They therefore take it upon themselves to make decisions for the people they recruit. When an individual's critical faculties are intact and fully functioning, information supplied by the destructive cult is meager. When the individual's critical functions are worn down and less operational, then the cult will supply more information. Deception includes outright lying, leaving out important information, or distorting information.[3] (Hassan, 99-100)

A former Moonie, "Jerry," shared his recollections about his recruitment with Dr. Mark Galanter. Jerry was invited by a young Japanese woman, to join a "discussion group" about world problems. In the group's van, Jerry heard someone use the word "Moonies" when speaking with the driver.

> Jerry: "Say, does the Divine Principle have something to do with the Moonies?"
>
> SHE: "You mean the Unification Church?"
>
> Jerry: "I don't know. Are they related?"
>
> SHE: "Reverend Moon wrote the Divine Principle."

Jerry: "Oh? Is he that Korean guy who spoke at Yankee Stadium?"

SHE: "Yes, he's a very wise man who gave us the ideas we've been talking about the last few days."

Jerry: "Oh, I see. How come you didn't mention it?"

SHE: "People criticize Reverend Moon unfairly, they would turn you away from joining the workshop, and you would lose the chance to hear his words. We just want you to have the chance to find out what he has to say."

Jerry did not remember being very surprised or distressed at this point. In fact, he gave surprisingly little thought to his growing involvement with a system of beliefs likely to have a profound influence on his life.[4] (Galanter, 51-3)

Jerry had effectively joined even before he realized the group's identity. The transition from his old, vaguely idealistic view (a general support for the world's poor) changed to an engagement in the new church's deviant beliefs without Jerry's even noticing. Jerry admitted to Galanter that he would *not* have gone to the workshop if he had known the Unification Church was behind it.[5] (Galanter, 52) "Proponents of unpopular belief systems have long revealed only what they felt wise during initial recruitment."[6] (Galanter, 53)

According to Singer, cult recruitment generally takes place – just like Jerry's – in four stages: an approach by a recruiter; an invitation; the first contact with the cult, where you feel special and loved; and the followup, where well-honed persuasive techniques are used to ensure greater commitment. Now, take a close look at an Amway Motivational Organization.

Step One: Contacting the Prospect

Imagine that I am an excited, new distributor. My AMO sponsor or leader helps me refine my recruitment approaches, and identify weak spots in my prospect – you! My own experience is expressed by Singer: "There is no limit to the ingenuity and also the trickery used. *Former cult members often tell me that they didn't even notice their first fatal step toward joining because so much deception was involved.*"[7]

On a tape widely used throughout several AMOs, *The Basics of Contacting and Inviting* (DBR474), Diamond Tim Bryan explains:

But, the important thing is to make sure that when you use the approaches, you use them properly. Sometimes you can take a very simple approach and by changing a few words, you deny yourself the usefulness of that approach because you make a mistake.[8] (DBR474)

An AMO distributor/recruiter must be letter-perfect smooth.

Initially, distributors contact and invite only people they already know. (See the section below on *Making the List*.) Once they have run through all their family, friends, acquaintances, people from church, people they work with, people they attended high school or college with, then they seek fresh blood. They must learn to meet strangers, contact them, and entice them to see the marketing plan. My sponsor guides me through all this.

Singer describes a typical cult recruiting process, one which is readily applicable to an Amway recruitment. First, I – as the recruiter – must learn something about the prospect to convey the notion that recruiter and prospect have something in common. Then I must appear to be caring and interested. Finally, I demonstrate that I have "something to offer by extending a verbal invitation to an event, a class, or a dinner."[9] (Singer, 110)

As a distributor/recruiter, I am routinely taught to meet people – in malls, restaurants, grocery stores, in the workplace, in churches, anywhere there are people. But once I meet them, what do I say to them? The upline teaches me to talk about **family, organizations, recreation,** and **money** (or **message**). "Memorize the first letters of these four words," my sponsor tells me, "*FORM*." These "spontaneous" conversations, held anywhere with anyone, give me the information I later use to entice my prospect.

But I still need to *get motivated* to meet people. Yager's tool list includes many teaching tapes on contacting and inviting. On a sheet of tools recommended for use by brand-new distributors, one AMO lists more than a dozen teaching tapes and videos which discuss nothing but "contacting and inviting."

One tape that teaches how to contact new prospects is GCS 103, *It's Called Practice*. The speaker is Bo Short, a Diamond Direct Distributor.

"Scuse me, could you help me? By the way, my name's Bo Short. What's your name? 'Jeff.' Nice to meet you. Are you from around here? 'No, I'm from Oklahoma.' Get out of town, are you serious? Forget what I wanted to ask you about, maybe you can help me out. This is a fluke! I'm

in the process of expanding a business in the Oklahoma market, and basically I'm looking for a go-getter type. Do you know anybody like that? 'Well, I'm pretty ambitious.' Look, I don't have time to talk right now, but if you'll write your name and number down on the back of this card, I'll give you a call when I get a chance. Hey, Jeff, it was nice to meet you. I'll give you a holler when I get a chance.

"The approach is nothing more than asking for directions. Except instead of asking for directions to the mall, you're asking for directions to an ambitious person's house."[10] (GCS103)

Of course, no matter where the contact is from, Short points out, he or she can help you out, as you are "expanding a business" anywhere they happen to mention.

Step Two: Inviting Your Prospect to See The Plan

Nobody joins Amway without seeing the circles first. As a new recruit, I invite you – a relative, a friend, an acquaintance – to my home for an evening. But I won't mention Amway – not when I contact you; not when I invite you to the meeting; or even when the meeting starts. Instead, my objective is to get you all to look at the "business opportunity" without disclosing what it is.

Here are some of Yager's suggestions from his book (promoted throughout the organization as "The Bible of building your successful Amway business").

- I've started my own business...
- I'm working with a group of top-flight people to put together some income advantages for paying the higher costs of education and even retiring a lot sooner than they could otherwise...
- What is it? A professional distribution business.
- What's the name? My own company. (Give it a name)*
- Who is it? A group of independent businesspeople.

That is all. You should never try to explain anything more over the telephone or in person.[11] (Yager, 230)

---

* Remember Hassan's statement: "The practice of deception by destructive cults extends to the use of various 'front organizations' to confuse potential recruits. . ." Hassan, p. 100.

Above all, when you are prospecting, contacting and inviting, don't be a *SAP!* In other words, don't talk about *Selling And Products* at first. ... If they prejudge and close their minds to the full potential, everyone loses.[12] (Yager, 251)

Over and over again, speakers on tapes and at Seminars & Rallies, Introductory Seminars, and major functions drum into distributors' minds the phrase "Never mention *Amway, Products or Selling* when you are talking to a prospect." Of course, you shouldn't lie, they say. If the prospect comes right out and *asks* you "Is it Amway," don't lie to him. But still there are ways of answering that question without admitting that it's Amway – answer a question with a question, distributors are taught.

"Is it Amway?" "Why, what do you know about Amway?"

"Is it Amway?" "Are you talking about the 'old' Amway or the 'new' Amway?"

"Is it Amway?" "It's my own business, X and Z Enterprises."

"Is it Amway?" "Are you thinking of the selling products door to door thing?" "Yes." "No, this is the Amway network system that deals with MCI, satellite dishes, car sales, home mortgages, etc. Your involvement would be in the networking aspect of the business."

"Is it Amway?" "What do you know about Amway?" "I know I don't want to sell stuff to my friends." "No kidding, niether do I! What you're thinking of is Phase I, I'm involved in Phase III. . ."

The list goes on and on and on.

Bryan explains on tape:

We believe in the curiosity approach and you need to understand something. There are two sides to the business. There is a corporate side and then there is a system side, the networking side. What we are trying to do is get people curious, interested, and excited about the side of the business that we participate in. That is the international network marketing system and its development. So, when we talk to people, we want to get them curious about the networking side, not the corporate side.... We have no intention of ever deceiving anybody when it comes to an approach. But, we think sometimes it can be an exception when you let people know it is Amway because you let them hear the corporate side of the business and when they think of that, they think of a company that had a bad reputation and that is simply a direct sales network, selling basically a very narrow line of products called cleaning products. And we think that if you let a person know that, you are deceiving them as to what really the main thrust of what we're trying to do is, and that is "the system".[13] (DBR474)

Here is some teaching on how to invite prospects to see the plan. This comes from Double Diamond Randy Haugen, on the same tape.

'*John, this is Randy. I'm looking at an idea that looks very interesting. I'd like to get together with you and get your input on the details.' Another one would be, 'John, I'm involved in a project that I think you will be interested in. Let's get together and go over some of the details.' Here is another one. 'John, I've run into someone who is making a lot of money in a networking concept. I need someone with a good head like you to take a look at the details and see if you can find a flaw.' 'John, I've run across something that is going to mean a lot of money. I'd like to get together and talk about the possibilities.' 'John, I know you are pretty sharp and I've always respected you. I need you to give me your input on a business idea.' Here's one last one that I've got for you, I was just goofing around with the other day and I did this and it worked so good that I thought I would share it with you. 'John, I'm working on a secret project. I would like to get the four of us together and talk about the possibilities.' This is one that you can use to call for someone else and all you've got to do on this one is say something to the effect of, 'John, have you ever heard of a guy named', whatever you want to use - somebody in your upline, I'll just give you the one I've got here. 'John, have you ever heard of a guy named Randy Haugen?' 'No.' 'He's involved in networking and he deals with MCI, satellite dishes, Mastercard, home mortgages, furniture, electronics and about five thousand other things. He is semi-retired at the age of 33 and he is teaching me how he operates. I'm looking for a couple of key people. Now, this is not an offer, but let's take an hour and get together and cover the details and when we get all done, I'll know if I have an interest in you and you'll know if you have an interest in it.'*[14] (DBR474)

Or for a different approach to inviting your prospect, use **Ad Packs**! The Ad Pack consists of a **generic** tape and **generic** literature: these carefully sculpted marketing tools never mention Amway, but instead talk about the poor state of the economy, the uncertain futures of all employees and traditional business owners, and promote "a business of your own" as the only way to "succeed" today. Of course, this business of your own must meet certain guidelines, which just happen to coincide with the profile of an Amway distributorship as it is promoted by the AMO: unlimited upward mobility, small initial investment, freedom to develop it in your spare time, and so on.

My own invitation to see the plan provides a typical example of the deceptiveness of the recruiting: a telephone call from my neighbor, a request to help him "evaluate" a "business opportunity" because he "respects my judgment."

Does a novice question his sponsor about the apparent deceptiveness of the prospecting and contacting process? Then the upline will explain, "George, if we tell them that it's Amway, that's when we're deceiving them! Maybe their only experience of Amway was some little old lady in tennis shoes coming around to sell them a box of SA8™ (Amway's brand of laundry detergent). So if you say to them, 'I'm in the Amway business,' they think of that little old lady. They know they don't want to go door to door, so they won't look at your opportunity. And yet, if they came and saw what you have to offer with an open mind, they would see the potential and get involved. So you see, if we tell them it's Amway, that's when we're deceiving them."

I wonder how it would work if a U.S. Army recruiter came into the local high school and used a technique like that. "Hey, son, what are your plans after you graduate?" "Are you a recruiter for the Army?" "Why, do you want to join the Army?" "No, I want to go to college and become a genetic scientist." "Well, we have just the program for you. We need to sit down and talk." No, the recruiter goes into the school wearing his uniform, with every button, bar, and ribbon shining and polished. Everyone knows who he is and what he's there for, and those students who are not interested in joining the military don't waste their time or his.

Step Three: Showing The Plan

Let's look at a home meeting, where the circles are being shown. Showing the plan, or "spinning the circles", whether in a one-on-one setting, a home meeting, or an Introductory Seminar, always follows the same basic format, dictated by the AMO leader. This is how Yager outlines it:

Introduction

The performance begins *before* the meeting opens. Our **marker man**[**]
(the one who draws the circles) will chat with the prospects, finding out as
much as he can about their families, jobs, recreation, and other possible
"hot buttons." Then the host will introduce the speaker. saying something
like, "It's my pleasure to introduce Marvin Markerman. Marvin is incredibly successful with this business concept that he's going to be sharing with
us all tonight. He's a real good friend of mine, and I know you'll be
excited to hear what he has to say." In reality, he first met Marvin two
days ago, he has no idea whether he's successful or not except that he's
been instructed to tell the prospects that Marvin is successful, and he's not
even really sure himself if he trusts this guy. Marvin is introduced as a
good friend who is successful, and the prospects will be excited. In an
Introductory Seminar, the marker man will be introduced by a Direct Distributor. The introduction will take longer, but the content is the same.

The Dream

Next is the **Dream Session**. This will typically last longer than all the
rest of the presentation combined. This is where the speaker talks to the
prospects about goals and then discusses some common "hot buttons."
(Think about your own hot buttons. Can they be punched? What about:
travel? private and/or college education for your kids? a nicer home?
luxury cars, boats, jewelry? early retirement?) The Amway dream includes
them all. Plus, as a sop to those with social consciences, charitable
donations.

If the marker man does his job properly, he involves the prospects by
inviting their participation. "Imagine that you've just won a $10 million
lottery." Or, "You know those letters you get in the mail from Publisher's
Clearing House, or Ed McMahon? What would you do if..." By the end of
the dream session, prospects are usually mesmerized. They are leaning

---

[**]   It is almost never a "marker woman." The majority, about 80% of all
      North American distributors, are married couples who are taught early that
      it is the man's job to show the plan. When I was a single distributor, I
      showed many plans. The minute I married, my upline strongly discouraged
      me from doing this. It was my husband's job, and he needed to do it in
      order to enhance his self-respect, we were told.

forward in their seats, smiling, eyes slightly glazed. They don't realize the speaker has been using a trance-inducing mind-control technique called **guided visualization** or **guided imagery**. If he's really good, he will also have been using a technique known as **voice rolling** or **pacing and leading** to speed up your trance. Often the marker man is not even aware he is using these techniques: he's just doing it the way his upline taught him.

What is this all about? This is about the state of the listener's mind – *your* mind. When you are functioning normally, you have a sense of reality which serves as your backdrop and frame of reference for activities and experiences. This reality framework can be diminished or even eliminated. Guided imagery might be the technique to accomplish it.

The result is *trance*. Temporary trance states are induced – by design – in many cults, in order to make recruits and members more amenable to suggestion. **Naturalistic trance induction** is a trance brought about through an indirect method of hypnosis, such as the careful use of language and method of speaking (pacing and leading).

One interesting method of trance induction is to use speech filled with contradictions. The message is simply not logical, so of course you can't follow it. But the presentation overwhelms you and can actually detach you from reality.

Indirect trance induction can also be accomplished through storytelling. Cult leaders combine repetitive, rhythmic speaking techniques with storytelling. The listeners are urged to stop analyzing, and just picture the images the speaker is presenting. "Picture yourself on the upper deck of a beautiful cruise ship…" If the content doesn't get you, the emotions – yours, and those of others around you – will.

When the trance has set in, you won't blink or swallow as frequently, and your facial expression will be blank or neutral. The trained speaker looks for those symptoms. Once he sees them, he knows that he has accomplished his purpose. Whatever he's selling, he can sell now!

The Two-to-Five-Year Plan

Our speaker (and what business does he represent? We still don't know.) quickly outlines some of the incomes available through his "opportunity," and contrasts that with "the rut," or what you can expect to accomplish through your job or traditional business. Then he moves through the numbers of the (unidentified) Sales and Marketing Plan extremely rapidly. The prospects still don't know he's talking about Amway at this point, and the meeting has been going on for about an hour. At a recent Introductory Seminar, which lasted for one hour and fifteen minutes, the word "Amway" was not mentioned until one hour and seven minutes had passed.

History of Amway Corporation and the System

Following the circles, the speaker spends perhaps five minutes on the history of the corporation, finally announcing that the opportunity he's talking about was put together by the Amway Corporation. This is the first time the word "Amway" is used. Immediately following, he launches into a description of the **system** and talks about the upline. He shows Diamond **lifestyles**, either through a video or a book titled *Profiles of Success* which is filled with "success stories" and photos of Diamonds and higher levels. Featured are large homes, luxury cars, boats, airplanes, enormous rings, flashy necklaces, and all the other "rewards" of being a successful Diamond Direct Distributor. Yager recommends spending at least twice as long on this part of the plan as on the discussion of Amway. These lifestyle tools are used in every AMO with which I am familiar, even though Amway's rules prohibit the use of lifestyle materials in recruiting.

Stephen Butterfield, a distributor for two years during the 1980's who later wrote a book entitled *Amway: The Cult of Free Enterprise*, includes a chapter called "Starting Right".

> The ideal way to be sponsored in my line was according to a prescribed series of steps: the new prospects first attend a get-together to see the Plan. Never call this a 'meeting.' The guests might smell out commitment emanating from the very texture of the word. No one should hear or guess the word 'Amway' until the... end.[15]

In fact, distributors who attend the meeting are instructed not to discuss anything business-related before the meeting starts, lest the dreaded A-word accidentally be spoken in the hearing of a new prospect.

Now, notice that less than 25% of the time is spent discussing the Sales and Marketing Plan and Amway Corporation. It is not uncommon for new prospects to be confused when the meeting is finally over. They understand there's some connection between Amway and what the speaker has been discussing, but they have no idea that they will sign an Amway Distributor Application if they get involved.

Step Four: Followup

The object of showing the Plan once is to get it in front of the new couple twice... The cardinal rule is to follow up within two days... At the second Plan-showing the distributor says to his prospects, "There are a few things you need to know in order to be successful in this business." He does not ask if the couple are getting in... he has already made the decision for them. If they make a decision, it will have to be to resist him.

One thing I must ask is that you have complete confidence in everything I do and say. The demand for 'complete confidence' is much more than a sales technique... it is central to the whole Amway business. If the prospect could foresee where this demand leads, she might jump up from the table and hustle her would-be sponsor out into the street.[16] (Butterfield, 48-9)

The object of showing the plan, your sponsor will tell you, is to get it in front of the prospects a second time. Do your prospects know that? Absolutely not. Nevertheless, "If you do a meeting without booking another meeting from it," your upline teaches, "you've wasted a night."

Ideally, if you've played your cards right, your prospects will agree to let you come to their house and "expose the concept" to *their* prospects while they are seeing it the second time – fast work! And as soon as the prospect hosts his first house meeting, he is ready for the kit, according to system teaching. The Amway Business Kit contains literature, plus Amway products. Cost is $151.00 in the United States.

Amway does not require a new distributor to purchase the product portion of the kit, which includes 12 products and five dispenser bottles costing $58.26. But almost no distributor is willing to split a kit and be stuck with $100 worth of products, so a new distributor in reality must purchase the entire kit. Moreover, each AMO has its own additional "business kit" that the new distributor must buy when he signs up "if you want to succeed." "The tools are optional," he is told, "but so is success."

When I was sponsored, nobody asked me if I was ready to get in, if I wanted the kit, or when I wanted the kit. My upline simply brought it into the house following my first meeting with prospects. This is called having an "assumptive attitude." Yager advises:

Do not ask, 'Are you getting in?' or 'What have you decided?' Instead, assume that the prospect is ready to get started. Ask questions that cannot be answered with a simple 'yes' or 'no'.[17] (Yager, 275)

One diamond routinely counsels, "Prospects need to be led. They don't want to make a decision themselves." "Assume they're getting in. If they don't want the kit, they will have to tell you 'no'." This takes much more strength of will and of mind than most people have. "After all," the prospect thinks, "these people are so nice, so friendly, and they really care about my future. I would just be hurting their feelings if I turned them down after all the effort they've put in. I'll get in and try it for a while."

It should be noted that an "assumptive attitude" is a characteristic of most successful salespeople. Any sales organization is in the business of manipulating people's decisions, but most are not cultic. It's only when the salespeople manipulate those decisions *and* take control over other unlrelated decisions in the person's life, entice them into the organization through an organized process of deception, and remove them from their social framework that one begins to question whether the organization is cultic. Using a particular sales technique, by itself, does not turn a business into a cult.

The List

When do you make the list? As soon as your sponsor thinks you are teachable, and certainly by the time you get your kit. "The list" is a list of your prospects' names, addresses and phone numbers." Make a duplicate list with carbon paper," you are told. Why? So that if you should decide not to go ahead and build the business, your erstwhile sponsor will go after every prospect on that list himself. You will be told things like, "If you're out of names you're out of business," or "You need to have a big list. If you have a list with 100 names on it, you will be much more confident in calling people and approaching people. But if you only have five names, you won't have the confidence to approach them properly and you'll be out of business very quickly." Don't worry – you'll have lots of help making your list.

I was taught to use copies of the *Amagram*, Amway's monthly distributor magazine. One section of the magazine shows pictures of new direct distributors. We called it the "funny pages." We would open to the "funny pages," and start going through the names and locations to jog the new distributor's memory. "Who do you know named Nancy? Jane? Bob? Henry? Who do you know from Boston, Massachusetts? From Long Island? From Colorado Springs? Who do you know who's a dentist? A building contractor? A teacher?" There are a number of tapes that deal exclusively with the process of making this list. Prospects are taught to put *everyone* on the list, regardless of where they live or how many years it's been since they've been in touch. "Go through your old high school yearbook," you are told, "your college annual, your guest list from your wedding..."

There are several reasons why your sponsor will take such pains with you over your list of names. First, in case you turn out to be a "loser," a "wimp," a "quitter," or "immature," and actually decide not to build the business, your sponsor will have your names list so he can approach all your friends, relatives and acquaintances on his own behalf. Second, the activity of making the list pulls you into a deeper involvement in the business. The more time you invest, the more likely you are to stay involved long enough to get hooked on tapes. Third, it is a way for the upline to continue to take over your time – and, remember, control of the recruit's time and environment is a key ingredient to successful cult recruiting.

Now that you've made the list, held at least two home meetings, and purchased your kit, you are no longer a "prospect" but a "distributor." Does this mean you now have all the information you need to successfully develop an Amway business? Not by a long shot. This information will be provided gradually, but the more amenable you are to changing your belief system, the more quickly information will be provided.

Is Amway a cult? The Amway business *by itself* does not appear to be. But the recruiting process, *as practiced and taught by the AMOs*, is certainly deceptive. Let's look at some other criteria in Chapter Twelve.

TWELVE: Deceptive Mind Control at Functions

By analyzing transcripts of Introductory Seminars, Seminars & Rallies, and major functions, it is easy to find specific examples of the deceptive mind-control used at AMO meetings. Here we will summarize the major areas that speakers manipulate. Keep in mind that all the speakers at these functions will be Direct Distributors or above.

Introductory Seminars

At an Introductory Seminar, speakers have been well trained to make themselves more "relatable" to the audience in several ways:
* If it's **negative**, say it about yourself.
* If it's **positive**, say it about the prospect.

Speakers disarm the audience by warning them in advance that they're going to have to change their thinking. This actually causes prospects to relax and *suspend* their critical thinking.

Speakers have been taught to use faulty logic to get the audience to change its perceptions and beliefs. The most common "non-logic" goes something like this: If I am wealthy, I must be intelligent. Since I am intelligent, I have something to teach you. Since you are not "intelligent" (i.e., rich), you have *nothing* to teach me and are of no value to society. You are stupid and only I (and other "intelligent," upline speakers like me) can teach you. (Of course, to make themselves relatable while they call you names, they put it in terms of a third person. "When I was a dumb broke loser, I met this intelligent rich guy...") Here's how one Diamond phrased it, describing when he first saw the plan:

> The guy that made the presentation got up in front of us told us that 'let me assure you of something ladies and gentlemen, there's a doctor, a lawyer, an accountant and an architect here tonight and I assure you that every one of them are far in excess of me in intelligence and education to the point that they're overeducatedly **stupid!!** Unless you make 60,000 bucks a month...'[1] (Diamond Dave Humphrey)

Other examples of flawed logic include:

* Millionaires think a certain way. "We" think that way. In order to become a millionaire you must think as we do.[2] (Humphrey)
* You must change your environment to eliminate all negative. ("Negative" is anything we don't want you to hear or know.)
* Trading time and effort for dollars is bad. "I was trading hours for dollars. Even though I was making a lot of money, when I was there I made money. When I wasn't, I didn't make any money. That's the time limiting factor... How many of you all make money when you don't work at all?"[3] (Diamond Jim Hayes)
* Since I am successful and I dress and look a certain way (no facial hair, for example), then in order to be successful you must dress and look this way, too.[4] (Humphrey)
* You must become rich and successful **now**. Otherwise, you'll be old and broke, or dead within months of retiring from your J-O-B.[5] (Humphrey)
* Amway distributors are *free*. Dave Humphrey claims, "I like to think of myself as somewhat of an oddity in America. I said, 'I'm rich, I'm young and I'm free. End of conversation.' "[6] (Humphrey)
* Amway **winners** have peace of mind.
* Amway **winners** benefit their fellow man.

Speakers will create an "us-versus-them" attitude. "I'm rich and free, they're poor and slaves. But if you'll do what I tell you to do, you can be counted with the 'rich and free' group and look down on those poor broke losers." In the outside world, "they" are

- losers
- stuck
- bad managers
- lazy

You don't want to be a loser, do you? Then the only way to become a winner is through this plan. You must make a commitment to become successful (only through this plan), and not look back.

If you're attending this meeting as a prospect, you don't realize that the majority (often 70% or more) of the people in the room are not prospects like yourself, they are distributors who have been well trained in how to behave at the Introductory Seminars. They will smile, laugh and clap when the speaker expresses attitudes and ideas that might normally be very offensive to you. The *peer pressure* will effectively draw you closer to their way of thinking, without your even realizing it.

Another proven way to get people to suspend their critical thinking and simply accept what's said is to make illogical, confusing statements. An examination of a written transcript of an Introductory Seminar shows this very clearly. But when you're in the audience listening, the lack of logic short-circuits your ability to weigh and analyze what's being said.

Introductory Seminars never begin with the facts. They begin with the dream, with personal anecdote, and some highly illogical discussion of economics and wealth. The actual business plan is saved until the end, after your defenses have been broken down. While incomes are shown, there is no mention of expenses – which we know to be significant – aside from the minimal "investment" required to purchase a starter kit.[7] The "numbers" are done very rapidly. To distract you, speakers will often make jokes about how illegible their handwriting is as they scrawl figures, and erase them quickly. The name "Amway" is never mentioned until the very end of the meeting. Typically, if the meeting lasts an hour and a quarter, the Amway name will be dropped at about minute 68 or 70. Immediately after mentioning Amway, the speaker will launch into a description of the "proven success system" that he's a part of, and that you, too, can join if you choose to leave the ranks of the stupid broke losers and become a winner.

Athena Dean, in her book *All That Glitters Is Not God*, describes the MLM (Multilevel Marketing, sometimes known as "network marketing" or "network distribution") opportunity meetings she used to hold for new distributors. Her meetings followed the AMO model, and her description is applicable to Introductory Seminars, and compelling:

> First I got people excited about the opportunity... I showed them graphically how bad their current situation was. I emphasized how their bills were either being paid late or not at all. I pounced on their lack of hope and magnified their fears. Then I began sowing seeds of discontent. Even if their jobs got better or they got a raise, could they match what I had to offer? Of course not.

> Once I had painted a grim picture of their lives, I offered to rescue them from their terrible financial trap with my product and program. I eroded the credibility of corporate America by raising fear-based possibilities of mergers, takeovers, cutbacks, layoffs, transfers, demotions, and unfair evaluations. I also knew how to convincingly discredit small business and discourage owning any kind of franchise.

> Once I had them convinced they had no freedom, no independence, and no joy, I raised fear for the future. I targeted retirement and blasted away at their security. I reminded them of important things in life... Finally I convinced them MLM is a way of life they could trust. I learned how to effectively and convincingly make them want what I offered and become discontent with what they had.[8] (Dean, 1999, 71-2)

Seminars and Rallies

Deceptive mind control doesn't stop with the Introductory Seminar – not at all. Think of all the monthly Seminars & Rallies that you, as a distributor, will attend! The AMO's expressed agenda for the Seminar & Rally is to teach you how to build your business. Under it lies the hidden agenda. What is that? Deception, and money. As demonstrated in earlier chapters, distributors are continuously deceived. They are deceived about the investment required in the business, the time frame needed to reach a level of profitability, about the profit potential, and about the true source of wealth displayed by their leaders. Leaders mislead, and often lie outright, about the profitability of the motivational tool and function business, while they live lavishly off the hopeful distributors' "investments" in the tools.

To further this hidden agenda, speakers have been taught ways to disarm any skepticism, to edify the system and its leaders (and by association, themselves), and meanwhile guide you to covet many glittering dreams. Your attitude must be made upbeat and positive: they work on that. In fact, one cultic ploy has always been to separate you from information and from former social support groups. Therefore, the AMO simply labels your friends and family (those who are **losers** and don't join the business) as negative and teaches you to avoid them. News programming and other sources of information that aren't filtered through the AMO leaders are also negative. The motivational tools come into play too, both to promote the agenda and to fill the ever-widening gaps as you leave your former activities and friends.

Your appearance, your spouse, your children, must fit the image of the perfect Amway family. This is pounded in. The speakers recommend books like *Dress for Success* and *You Are What You Wear*. "Get rid of the facial hair," the men are told. "Studies have shown that many people don't trust men with facial hair. Don't hurt your business by hanging onto that beard or mustache." Women are told they must wear skirts or dresses when building the business. "This is a business of duplication," the speaker announces, "but whatever you do will be duplicated a little bit less. Men, you need to wear a dark suit, a white shirt, and a tie with a touch of red. Ladies, you might have a really sharp-looking pantsuit that looks great. But if you wear that to a meeting, some other gal might decide to show up in slacks and a casual shirt. Next thing you know, the women are coming to meetings wearing cut-off shorts and halter tops, and that's not good business. So, for business, we recommend skirts or dresses. And watch those necklines and hemlines too! Your neckline shouldn't be too low, your hemline shouldn't be too high. Don't advertise it if it's not for sale!"

Your children must be **positive** about the business, and the woman speaker will spend several minutes during the seminar instructing distributors on how to bribe their kids into compliance with Mom and Dad's new Amway lifestyle. Young children should be taught to cut out pictures of things they want from Amway's *Personal Shopper*® Catalog and put them up on the refrigerator. Then, on the child's calendar, Mom and Dad stick stars or points for every time little Johnny or Susie behaves for the babysitter. When enough stars are accumulated, the parents buy the item for the child. Variations on the same scheme are recommended for older children.

You must do everything the way winners do! You have to learn to walk like a winner (did you know that winners walk 20% faster than other people? That's what my upline told me!) and talk like a winner (winners talk fast because they're excited), dress like a winner and rush around like a winner. You also must also buy! buy! buy! Amway products. Selling products is not promoted much, but buying for yourself (called self-usage) is a must – to the tune of anywhere from $400 - 1500 per month![9] Of course, buying tools and attending functions are also necessities, stressed by every speaker.

> Do you realize that Amway today, is the answer to the world's problems, and you're a part of all of this? [clapping, cheering] This is more than just a business, but it's a way of changing your life, it's a way of changing your kids' lives, and it's a way of changing your world.[10] (Diamond Jerry Manzi, PS77)

Seminars & Rallies usually feature a speaker couple* who can be Directs, Sapphires, or Emeralds. Occasionally Diamonds speak at these functions. The Seminar portion of the function is where the teaching takes place. But like any other AMO function, it ends with a **dream** session, filled with guided imagery to cloud your critical thinking and lessen the chances that you might analyze what was said before it.

The Rally portion is billed as the "fun" part of the day, where the speakers get to tell their "story." They talk – briefly – about what their lives were like before the business. Usually, since this is negative, the wife covers the "before" section. Then the husband talks about the "good stuff," which has all happened since they joined the business. Their true story will be revised before they tell it, saving all the positive for after they joined the Amway business and avoiding any negative.

Do you in the audience have any guilt or fear? Do you love your children and want the best for them? These emotions will be manipulated by the speakers.

---

* It's almost always a couple. If by any chance there is an unmarried distributor at the Direct Distributor level, he or she will be paired up with another single of the opposite sex, or will share the stage with a married couple.

The evening finishes with – you guessed it – another dream session. An intense session of guided imagery sets your dream, once again, before your dazed eyes. And just think – you get to come to another one next month!

Major Functions

All the ones that just wanted to diddle and piddle stayed at home, right? [audience cheers] *All the ones that wanted to give it a try left early.* [audience cheers] *All the ones that just wanted to hit 4000 left about 20 minutes ago.* [audience cheers] *Now we got the ones that are ready to go direct, right?* [audience cheers] *All right! WHOO! Okay. I forgot one part, I guess, or did I say that at the beginning. All the ones that didn't have any guts quit.* [audience cheers][11] *(Triple Diamond Jerry Meadows, SOT 308)*

As you would imagine, the same heavy mind-control techniques are used at the major functions, with a few additions to the arsenal. These events are touted as life-changing, and indeed they are! Everything normal is torn apart, beginning with time.

You left your children with a babysitter for the weekend. You left work early on Friday, or took the day off in order to drive for hours – three, eight, twelve hours or more. You skip dinner to get into the function on time. You're there until midnight or 1:00 AM. You're lucky to get to bed before 2:00 or 3:00 in the morning. Saturday morning you're up early for breakfast and the morning session from 9:30 or 10:00 AM to 1:00 or 2:00 in the afternoon with no breaks. You get a couple of hours for sightseeing (unless you're in an organization that holds Leadership Meetings during this time), then you're back in line for the evening session. This will go on until the small hours. (If it's a Free Enterprise, the major Yager function of the year, the hours are extended and the breaks are almost nonexistent.) If you want the speakers' autographs or pictures, you'll stand in more lines and be lucky to be in bed by 3:00 or 4:00 AM. Sunday morning, up early for the "non-denominational Christian worship service," with an offering, an altar call, and the "sermon" given by a Diamond. Then a Leadership meeting in the afternoon, before you drive home three, eight, twelve

They danced to the Goads, all those suits, three steps left then three steps right, etc., so that you are forced to participate.[12] (Internet)

hours or more. Many distributors arrive home just in time to pay the sitter, shower, change and go to work Monday morning.

Along with sleep deprivation during the weekend, your eating patterns and diet are also shot. You either skip meals, or eat junk food snacks for the whole weekend. Other factors are at work to disturb your natural equilibrium. The meetings are full of mind-numbing sound and lights. Live musicians – many of whom, like the band *The Goads* or *Dreamer,* are Amway distributors – demand your participation as you clap, sing along, sway, or perform choreographed actions to go along with a particular song. This causes you to hyperventilate and engage in repetitive motion, all of which induce a trance state. Each session during the weekend begins with these musical acts, and there will be at least one such segment in the middle of the session; longer sessions may have more.

Now add the deceptions perpetrated by the speakers, add peer pressure, add emotional manipulation, and you have the major AMO functions which take place at least four times each year.

THIRTEEN: My Amway Story

The Single Years

My core involvement with the Amway business lasted for about thirteen years. During the first six of those years, I was a single parent, struggling to make ends meet financially, to be both mother and father to my two children, and to build the business. About a year after starting in Amway, I packed up my children and my meager possessions and moved about 300 miles away, to the town where my parents live. It was a move that made sense for me in every way except for building the Amway business. I was still dedicated, loyal and hardworking. I attended monthly Seminars & Rallies faithfully, although it meant driving 300 miles each way to do so and leaving my children with a babysitter for the weekend. I bought the tape of the week, and the book of the month, and often ordered extra tapes or books. I showed the plan, I sponsored people, and I even sold some product. I attended all major functions, spending money and time I didn't have, and leaving my children with babysitters.

During this time, I changed jobs frequently. The business had taught me to have a total contempt for honest gainful employment, so if anything about a job wasn't to my liking, I would leave. Or my bosses would tire of my lack of commitment to their goals, and send me packing. I didn't worry – after all, I always had the business to fall back on, and one of these days I'd be rich and could pay off my debts, right?

I had no social life. My friends were all in the business, and most of them lived several hundred miles away from me. I showed the plan to any new friends I met. If they didn't join my business, I knew they weren't "real friends," and therefore were not people I should spend time with. The AMO had taught me to live a life of social isolation, without goals or purpose except what could be accomplished through Amway. I cried myself to sleep a lot.

For at least three years after my separation and divorce, I was too emotionally scarred from that experience to even consider dating. When I finally did want to, I couldn't find anyone who interested me. After all, if a man was a winner, he would already be in the business – and, if in the business, he would be crossline from me and therefore unavailable! I finally managed to break through this mental/emotional barrier. One man I dated could barely contain his loathing when he discovered I was an Amway distributor. He claimed his previous marriage had broken up because of his wife's Amway involvement. I laughed at him. Obviously, he didn't understand the business! Another man I dated agreed to go to a function with me, a Family Reunion. He was thoroughly appalled at what he saw, and was very concerned about where I was heading. I didn't listen to him, either. I decided that dating was a bore, and I was better off on my own.

After leaving yet another job, I was unemployed for several months, and was barely able to buy food for my family and gas for my car. I was three months behind in my rent. The repo man came to take my car, and I staved him off by writing a check which I prayed wouldn't bounce. I missed several monthly seminars and didn't have the courage to tell my sponsor to take me off of tape of the week. It was time for the annual pilgrimage to Mecca – yes, that's actually what we called it – to Free Enterprise Day in Charlotte, North Carolina with the Master Dreambuilder himself, Dexter Yager. I had no money, so I didn't go. My sponsor was seriously annoyed with me. The fact that I had no income and two children to feed didn't cut any ice with him.

Finally I found a job again – actually, two jobs. I started to drag myself out of the financial pit I had dug, and I didn't listen to the tapes when they came every week, just threw them in a box. I felt happier. I had been having conversations for several months with the associate pastor at my church, trying to convince him of the need for a singles ministry. I decided that if God meant me to be single, then I was going to have some fun. I joined a small community theater group, something I had always wanted to do, and got a chorus part in Gilbert & Sullivan's *The Sorcerer*. I was busy, but I felt like a human being again. In fact, I was having a ball. I met a lot of nice people, and I didn't mention Amway, products or selling to a single one of them!

Despite two jobs, rehearsals two evenings a week, and church choir, I was seeing more of my kids than I had for years. In the midst of this, I met a man at my church, a widower with two children who went to school with my two kids. He knew that I was an Amway distributor, and was willing to overlook it. We were married within three months – another whirlwind.

I had never made a conscious decision to quit the Amway business, I had just drifted away on a chain of circumstances. When I thought about it at all, it was with the belief that I could always go back when the timing was better for me. I felt guilty for the way I was letting down my upline, who had been so good to me over the years and had invested so much time and effort trying to help me become successful. I had nothing but positive feelings about Amway, and I was still exclusively using Amway products.

The Married Years: Back in the Business

Shortly after we were married, my husband came into the bedroom early one morning to tell me he was leaving for work. "By the way," he announced, "I grabbed a couple of tapes from that box you have. I thought I'd listen to them on the way to work."

I sat bolt upright, wide awake instantly. What tapes had he picked? This would be his introduction to the business, and if he listened to the wrong tape first he wouldn't understand it! In a panic, I jumped up to see which tapes he had in his hand. Uh-oh, I hadn't even taken these out of the cellophane wrappers. Hastily I ran to the box of tapes and scrabbled through it. I found a couple of first-night tapes and handed them to him.

"Why don't you listen to these first," I suggested. "These have some good introductory information on them. Those other tapes you picked out will probably make more sense after you listen to these." I couldn't believe he was going to listen to the tapes, especially since I hadn't ever promoted the business to him. I was acting casual, but inside I was bursting with excitement. With the two of us working together, we would build a *fantastic* business!

My husband was off and running. He devoured the tapes, listening to six, seven or eight a day. His questions exhausted me, but I refused to show him the marketing plan, although I'd been showing it several times a week for about five years. After all, when a couple builds the business together, showing the plan is the man's job and I didn't want to start off our business as a couple on the wrong foot! So we invited my sponsors out for the weekend to show my husband the plan. They came, he saw, he said, "yes, let's do it." We were excited!

We bought a ton of generic prospecting tapes, tapes that don't mention Amway anywhere. We contacted people and put out ad packs. We attended monthly Seminar and Rally. Fortunately, a new location had opened up in the organization, only a three-hour drive away so we could go up and back in one day. We showed the plan. We sponsored one couple, who split up just a couple of months after getting their kit.

We went to Family Reunion, where I got food poisoning but didn't complain because it would have been negative. We drove to Charlotte for Free Enterprise Day. We attended Fall Extravaganza. We were excited!

Both of us had been getting more and more tired of winters. We were no longer very comfortable in our church, and thought our new family needed a fresh start. The area we wanted to live in had no market for the type of work my husband does. Then we found out that several couples in our upline were moving to Florida, and we were invited to move with them. "If you'll come to Florida with us," our upline Direct said, "and if you're willing to be teachable and work hard, we'll have you qualified as Emeralds within two years." That was all we needed. We sold the house, packed up the kids, and moved south.

Two years later, we were nowhere near Emerald; in fact, we were nowhere near Direct. My husband's job skills were not much in demand, and we had chewed through our savings. I was doing a little freelancing, but I didn't really put much into it. After all, I was going to be free in the business soon, I didn't need to develop those contacts to sell those stories and get those assignments, did I? We decided to add to our family and have a child together. I got pregnant and miscarried. My grandfather, with whom I was very close, developed a fast-growing and inoperable cancer. I traveled north, on the heels of the miscarriage, to be with him when he died.

Back at home, I suffered debilitating bouts of depression. My husband and I constantly fought about the business. Our financial resources were gone, and I was working with several temporary agencies to bring more money into the household. I announced that I would not even consider having another child unless we were building the business, as I wanted the freedom to be a stay-at-home Mom. My husband was questioning everything about Amway, and I didn't want to hear it. "You have to take it on faith!" I would scream at him. "You're analyzing it to death. Just accept the fact that it works and do it!" "If you ask me that one more time I think I'll slit my wrists!" Our home wasn't the site of "Amascussions" or "Ambattles," it was full-fledged "Amwar."

We went to Introductory Seminars or monthly Seminars & Rallies and smiled.

"Hi, how're you doing?"

"Great. We're great!" Smile, and lie some more.

Finally, my husband promised that he would buckle down and "do whatever it takes" to get our business built, and he started "putting the pedal to the metal" to "get the job done." In a blaze of passion one summer morning, I conceived again. After a few months of concerted effort, our business ground to a halt. My temper tantrums expanded along with my growing belly. We had no medical insurance. Every week we got Standing Order Tape and PaceSetter tape, and we attended all the Introductory Seminars, Seminars & Rallies, and major functions. We didn't have a negative product in the house. After a few months of constant verbal abuse from me, my husband became very depressed and withdrawn. As my pregnancy dragged on – one week, two weeks, almost three weeks past my due date – I would cry and claim that "even this baby hates me and doesn't want to be born."

Inevitably, the baby arrived and has been a wonderful addition to our family. I became totally engrossed in caring for her and tried to ignore the outside world. We still attended all the functions, bought all positive products, and bought standing order tape and book of the month.

Shortly after this, my husband found a new job. He would be working in his field of expertise, but in the sales department. He thought that learning to sell in a conventional job might help him better present the Amway plan and convince people to join our business. I made it plain that, to me, his new job was just a temporary inconvenience to put food on our table until we became successful in the business. I made no attempts to be supportive about his job-related problems and stresses, which were great. We had nothing to talk about with each other except the children and the business, and discussions of the business almost always erupted into fights, tears, and recriminations. We were no longer prospecting, contacting, or showing the plan, but we still bought standing order tape and book of the month, and attended all the functions.

"Hi, how're you doing. Great to see you."

"Great to see you too! We're doing awesome, how about you?" Smile, and lie, and smile.

One day, when the baby was about a year old, I got a call from my upline Diamond. (I'll call them Dudley and DeeDee. Those are not their real names.) "I just wanted to know if you were planning on being at the Open tonight," she asked.

"Sure," I answered, wondering what the call was about.

"If you can spare the time, Dudley and I would like to talk with you afterwards. Can you come for coffee after the meeting?"

"Absolutely. I'll be there."

All day I was in suspense. What on earth could they want to talk to *me* about?

After the meeting that night, they offered me a job. "Just part-time," they said, "just two days a week or so." They wanted to expand their business internationally, and needed a coordinator in the office for that.

My husband and I discussed it, and decided that the opportunity to get close to our Diamonds was too good to pass up, even though I had not planned on working. I started to look for childcare for my one-year-old, and with stars in my eyes, I went off to work for my Diamond.

The Diamond Years: In the Golden Cage

My first months as the employee of a diamond were fun and exciting. I was getting an inside look at the Amway business. I talked on the phone with Amway Corporation staff, Emeralds, Pearls, Directs, and other Diamonds. I was respected and appreciated by distributors throughout the organization. When we attended monthly Seminar & Rally, the Directs all wanted to talk with me. I felt like a celebrity. At Family Reunion, I was introduced at the Silvers and Up Meeting, and spoke to them about the international business and its potential. Directs, Pearls, even Emeralds rushed to open doors for me, find me a seat, or provide transportation.

I purchased computers for the office, handled all aspects of international development, and took over production of all the organization's print materials. I bought myself a new computer so I could bring work home. Thousands of distributors knew my voice on Amvox. I was in close personal contact with several key Amway employees and with key employees at InterNET Services Corp., as well as some of the Yagers. I was important!

Our home was still an Amwar zone. My husband was more and more frustrated with his job, and I was still determined we would become successful Amway distributors. After all, I now had an inside track! I saw my Diamond several times a week, and spoke to him daily on the phone or via Amvox. I knew so well how he thought that I could compose business letters for him using the same language that he would use. If distributors had questions that needed to be referred upline to him, I could tell them, "Well, you'll have to talk with Dudley about that, but I suspect he would say. . ." and I would be right. I was learning to think like a Diamond – from there it wasn't a big step to becoming one. Was it?

My husband made no effort to build the business. His job exhausted him, and he wanted to be able to enjoy his children right then, not years in the future. The oldest was halfway through high school, the youngest becoming more interesting and fun every day. Besides, the attraction for him had always spending time with the people in the business, and he had plenty of opportunity to do that now that I was in with the in crowd!

At home, I shut my husband out. We bickered constantly over petty details. I felt betrayed that he wasn't building the business, and I let him know it. I threw myself into my job more and more, and what little emotional energy I had left went to the kids. My husband withdrew more and more, and may have been clinically depressed although he refused to seek treatment. I stopped all my creative outlets – writing, playing music, even listening to music. I couldn't seem to concentrate on anything. I felt as though I was functioning in a perpetual mental fog. The fights still erupted periodically, ending in accusations, tears, and then sullen silence on my side. Our marriage was a mess, and the children tiptoed cautiously, trying to avoid my smoldering outbursts. Something had to change.

We decided we needed to get some time away, time that did not include an Amway business function. We had always wanted to take a cruise, and we had an anniversary coming up. I found a theme cruise that interested me – a mystery! I have always loved mysteries, and we agreed this would be fun. It turned out to be more than fun, it was a pivotal point in my life.

I really got involved in this mystery. I followed each episode, I looked for clues, and ended up as the only successful sleuth at the end of the cruise. The prize – a free cruise! I was ecstatic. I recognized, finally, that my creativity *wasn't* completely gone as I had thought, and that I was still capable of putting two coherent thoughts together. And somehow my winning gave me some new stature in my husband's eyes. I had achieved something of value, not because of chance, or luck, but because I had ability.

On returning home, non-Amway friends and family were excited about our experience, and wanted to hear all about it. At the office, it was a different story. My coworkers and Diamonds were visibly bored. If the cruise didn't come from the Amway business, it was worthless in their eyes. I began examining more critically some things I had just accepted before, about them and about their business, and was not comfortable with the conclusions I was drawing.

My husband was still talking about building a business. He wasn't taking any action, he still had reservations about it, but he wouldn't acknowledge, "no, I'm not going to build the business." I begged him, pleaded with him to just tell me once and for all what he wanted to do. He wouldn't make a decision.

Shortly after this, the Diamond couple had a fight of their own, which had more long-reaching effects than they will probably ever know. In the aftermath, she turned on me and lashed out with a viciousness and a fury that I had never seen before. I was stunned, in shock, and totally devastated. I had poured my heart and soul into their business, worked as hard as if it were my own, and had in some ways looked after their interests more carefully than they had. I cried for weeks, mourning the loss of my illusions.

I decided that nothing would induce me to develop an Amway business in their group, but I still thought that Amway was a good opportunity.

The storm with DeeDee had blown over – they thought. I was afraid to leave the job, because the money was fairly good and I didn't feel competent to do anything else, although I knew I had to. But inertia took over, and I made no work changes. I did stop going to monthly Seminar & Rally, although my husband continued to attend, and I no longer listened to Standing Order Tape.

Then suddenly my job became more of a golden cage than ever. Dudley decided, with only two weeks notice, to send me to Athens for the market opening in Greece. I had never traveled. My only trips out of the US had been into Canada when I lived in the north, and travel was a huge hot button for me. My husband agreed to keep things together at home, I bought a "learn Greek in ten days" tape set, and we rushed my passport application through by paying extra fees. Before I knew what hit me, I was on my first trans-Atlantic flight.

Once in Athens, I swung into a frenzy of activity. I had arrived in the early evening. The next day, Sunday, I took the afternoon to do some sightseeing. After that, I worked about 18-20 hours a day. The leads from the organization poured in. I had left the office with a stack of them, and a rented laptop computer to keep track of everything. Once at the hotel, new faxes arrived day and night. I couldn't leave my room, even for five minutes, without finding new faxes under my door when I came back. I had to take my phone off the hook in order to sleep, as US distributors paid no attention to the time zone differences. I got up early, met with distributors and prospects all day, made myself available outside the room where the Introductory Seminars were being held back-to-back all day and half the night. After the last meeting finished, all the Diamonds and their representatives met until one or two in the morning. I was able to eat at least one meal each day, quite an accomplishment in those busy circumstances.

The first day that business kits went on sale, I sent an Amvox back home to the organization describing the scene to them, and telling them that they hadn't lived as distributors until they had seen a mob of people fighting to get their Amway Business Kits. My face showed up in the official InterNET Services Corp. video of the Greece opening. I knew I wasn't going to build the business myself, but I was caught in the spell again.

I came home to a family life that was still hell. We were coping with an extremely stressful situation involving one of our children, and my husband and I were at loggerheads again. I knew I couldn't continue working for the Diamonds much longer, but didn't know what else to do.

I decided to start my own business, offering some of the desktop publishing services that I was already providing for the Diamonds. I had the computer, I had the software, and I had the expertise. I just needed to find some clients. I mentioned to my chiropractor that I was going into business, and before I knew it, I had a contract to produce a four-color brochure for the chiropractic office. Nobody was more stunned than I. I did a few more jobs, and gained a couple of regular clients.

I had barely recovered from the Greece trip when Amway announced a market opening in Colombia, and the Diamonds decided to send me. I would fly to Bogota, and then a couple of days later Dudley would fly down to be on the scene himself. We also had several distributors in the organization who were attending the opening, so some of the problems I had in Greece would be solved by having more people there to share the load. Besides, it was a chance to get away from the family mess at home.

While in Colombia, I was appalled by the insensitivity I saw to the financial situations of the prospects. Colombia is a very poor country: the average person in 1996 earned the equivalent of about $180.00 US per month. Many new distributors had to take out bank loans to finance the purchase of their Amway Business Kit, which sold for roughly $100.00 US. Yet their sponsors, or the Diamond AMO leaders present, insisted that they buy tools, tape packs, and all the other accouterments of successful North American distributors.

A statement I'd heard from an InterNET employee in Greece came back to haunt me: "My mandate here is to sell tools." The penny dropped, and I finally realized that sponsoring new Amway distributors was just a front for the sale of motivational tools and functions.

Following the market opening in Colombia, there were some big changes in Dudley and DeeDee's office staff. I had recognized the travel opportunities as a golden chain, and my desktop publishing business was doing well. But fear, and greed for more travel, kept me working for the Diamonds.

My husband was still talking about building the business but taking no action. Finally he confessed that he was afraid that if he didn't build the Amway business, I would leave him. Since I had been pleading with him to give it up for about a year at this point, I was baffled. Finally the ugly truth came out: our upline Direct, who by this time had lost several automobiles and his house because he was so deeply in debt, had told my husband years before that I would leave him if he didn't build the business. My husband believed him, and let the fear fester. I was furious that he would have believed this ill-speaking Direct. I came to realize that, if our dreams were truly God-given, then He would provide the ways for us to achieve them. For myself, I had put my faith back in God where it belonged, and not in the Amway business.

I began something I had for years thought about: I started writing a mystery novel. My desktop publishing business was growing, and I was just going through the motions at work.

I had one more trip, to the country opening in the Philippines. This time I went with a new cynicism. While enjoying my time there, and especially the Filipino people I met, I knew I was there to sell something I no longer believed in. I had been doing the job long enough to handle it competently, and I represented my employer's interests appropriately, but I loathed the part I was playing.

The Internet: The Final Curtain

Shortly before the Philippines trip, a memo, which later appeared on Amway's World Wide Web site, was sent to the Diamonds. It discussed a "disgruntled internet activist" with an anti-Amway web site, who was really a "secret" consultant for Procter & Gamble in their lawsuits against Amway. Intrigued, I went on an internet search and found the site: Sidney Schwartz' *Amway: The Untold Story*. I expected some rabid, wild-eyed crackpot spouting lies, and found the idea of an anti-Amway site mildly amusing. Instead, I found thorough research, well-reasoned arguments, legal pleadings, and most especially, hundreds of letters from distributors and their families.

My first reaction was that the anti-Amway letters were from losers, wimps, people with job mentality, and other common, thought-stopping epithets we were taught to apply to those who left the business. As I read more, I was terrified to find there were other people who felt as I did. Did that make me a broke, wimpy loser, too? I searched out other so-called negative sites, and discovered *Amway Motivational Organizations: The Nightmare Builders*, and several others. They all told variations on the same theme: the Amway business, as practiced by AMOs, is fraught with deception, lies, half-truths, and coercive mind-control practices. It is a cult, and many thousands of people are harmed.

I saw it, I knew it, but I wasn't ready to believe it. I stopped looking at the sites. My husband immersed himself in the anti-Amway sites he was finding on the internet. Night after night he pored over them. "What do you want to wallow in all that negative for?" I grumbled at him. "Let's just let it go and move on."

Then I stumbled across some information about the tool bonuses my Diamond was receiving. I had known, of course, that the tool income comprised a major part of his earnings, but this was absolutely incredible: the previous year, his bonuses from Amway had amounted to less than 5% of his total income: the other 95% came from motivational tools and functions. I felt sick, believing that I had helped him steal from his distributors. I felt even sicker, knowing how long I had been sucked into the scheme while the evidence was in front of my nose. My days as a Diamond employee were numbered. We set my leaving date, and I also started to look at the internet sites again. I was getting angry.

I thought of all the times I had heard my upline tell me, "the tools will help you grow in the business." "I don't achieve my goals in the Amway business until I help a lot of other people accomplish their goals." "It's vital that you attend this Seminar & Rally. You never know when a speaker will say something in the way that makes sense for *you* and will propel you to diamond." "You can't afford to miss this major function. You'll set your business behind from six months to a year if you don't go." "Can you afford to lose $100,000 by *not* attending this function?" "You need to support your upline and buy books upline, not from the bookstore." "You need to support your upline and attend every Introductory Seminar, even if you don't have a prospect to bring." I saw these statements now for what they really are: self-serving, income-producing lies. "Why should you work at a job and buy someone else's wife a mink coat?" the upline would ask. "Build a business of your own and get the coat for your own wife!" They never tell you where the money really comes from for *their* wife's mink, if you follow their instructions about how to build the business. It is not purchased with profits from the sale of Amway products and services, it's from the sale of motivational tools – tools which they tell you they only provide to help you in your business, because they "love" you.

I was done: done with working for these thankless deceivers, done with any thought of building a distributorship. I decided I would start to publicize the lies, the abuses, and the deceptions that I had witnessed, and to help others avoid entrapment by the AMOs. I put up my own web site. I contacted some of the other anti-Amway site owners. I began researching cults. And, as my husband and I heard from others who had been harmed by their AMO experience, we started to heal.

We are very fortunate that our families have forgiven us for all the years of neglect and insensitivity from us, and those relationships are also healing.

I am happier now than I've been in years. I know now that it is the system that is flawed. I may have my own flaws, too, but I am definitely not a loser, wimp, weenie, immature, or any of the other AMO-cult words used to describe those who choose a non-Amway road. My fearsome mood swings are just mild blips now. My relationship with my husband is better than it's been since I can remember. We are learning, slowly, how to develop friendships with others – real friendships, not the superficial exchanges that masquerade as friendship inside the AMO. Our children are learning again that there is more than one path to success, and that success isn't defined just in terms of money and things. We have our lives back.

FOURTEEN: What Next?

If you've never been an Amway distributor, it may be hard to see where Amway Corp. ends and the Amway Motivational Organizations begin. They are two very distinct – but inter-related – entities. It might help to think in terms of a "family tree." Suppose your grandparents came to the United States from Italy. Of course, lots of other people came here from Italy at the same time. They all would have had a lot in common: a common language, common ethnic heritage, and so on. But there would have been differences, too, from family to family. Those differences would tend to increase with each succeeding generation. If you think of Amway Corporation as the common heritage, and each different family as an AMO, you will get closer to understanding the Amway business. To extend this analogy, it is the "families," or the AMOs, which carry the system into nearly all aspects of the Amway distributor's life, not the common heritage (the corporation). We've taken a brief look at the corporation, then the system, the functions it puts on, and the tools it creates.

During my years as a distributor, several people suggested to me that I was involved in a cult. Angrily I refuted them, and told them they just didn't understand this special business. But after several years of employment with my upline, after I finally understood how the money

Is There Life After Amway?

What happens to you if you decide to leave the AMO fold and quit the business? The AMOs have worked very hard to instill the fear – possibly even the phobia – that there is no possible life for you outside the sheltering arms of the organization. Ever since you started in the business you've been hearing that those who pursue a non-Amway path are losers, quitters, whiners, wimps, and that they are condemned to a life of J-O-B servitude. What really happens to the millions of distributors who have walked away?

> I never got to the circles that night, or any night thereafter. It was like dumping an ugly master off your back and no longer having to fear his spurs, or go sniffing after his carrot.[1] (Butterfield, p. 177)

> All is well with us. Everything is going so much better since we are not doing the Amway business. We have gotten so much further by concentrating on paying off our debt through hard work and perseverance. I think by the end of this year, I may be able to think about leaving my job and staying home with my youngest. We have been pretty much ignored by our upline. But that is something we fully expected.[2] (e-mail)

really flows, I slowly began to see the deceptions that AMO leaders have perpetrated to keep distributors like me from finding out the secrets of their "wealth." That led me to start studying cults and cultic relationships, and to share those findings with you.

If you've been looking at the Amway business, we hope this book has provided you with enough information to make a considered decision. If you're a distributor already (or you're concerned about someone who is), you're probably scratching your head at this point and asking, "what next?"

Do Some Evaluating

Evaluating the AMO system objectively, once you've become part of it, is nearly impossible. But here are some questions you can ask yourself: Was there anything about my recruitment that was deceptive?

1. Did my sponsor avoid telling me that I would be seeing a presentation for the Amway business before I actually saw the plan?

2. Did my sponsor invite me to a social function (lunch, dinner, barbecue, party) or for "Christian fellowship" and then show me the Sales & Marketing Plan?

3. Before I saw the Sales & Marketing Plan, did my sponsor give me any literature, audio or videotapes that dangled the carrot of "financial freedom" without mentioning Amway?

4. Did my sponsor invite me to an Introductory Seminar, and imply it was about "success principles" or an unnamed (or misnamed) business opportunity?

5. Was the name "Amway" mentioned only at the *end* of the presentation?

6. Did my sponsor or upline, as part of showing the Sales & Marketing Plan, use a tool like the *Profiles of Success* book or any lifestyles video tapes to demonstrate the "success" available to Amway distributors?

7. Has my sponsor or other upline distributor ever said to me, "We've found that most people think they understand the Amway business, but they really don't have a clue. So we believe that, if we *tell* them ahead of time we're talking about Amway, that's when we're really deceiving them."

8. When I asked about the investment required to build a "successful" Amway distributorship, did my sponsor or upline just feed me platitudes like, "Winners don't count the cost," "What difference does it make? Do you have any better way to get where you want to go?" or "Don't worry about it. There's no large capital investment required."

9. Does my upline routinely put down or make fun of "traditional" business, investment, and employment?

If your answer was *yes* to most of these points, you need to seriously evaluate whether you want to join or support and perpetuate such a system.

Here is another important question to ask yourself: **am I using personal relationships for gain?**

1. Did my upline insist that I contact close friends and family to show them the plan?

2. Did my upline insist on getting a copy of my names list, so that *he* could contact my close friends and family?

3. Has my upline ever told me to "flush" any friend or family member who does not join my business?

4. Has my upline ever told me to avoid friends or family members who don't join my business, because they're negative?

5. Has my upline ever instructed me to forego family gatherings for holidays or important occasions like weddings, graduations, anniversaries, birthdays, or bar or bat mitzvahs in order to attend an AMO function?

6. Has my upline ever told me, "Your friends/family don't pay your bills, and they've already shown they don't understand this business by not getting in. You don't need to take advice from them."

7. When I meet new people, do I always have a recruitment agenda in mind?

8. If I belong to a church, have I ever approached other church members and invited them to look at Amway as a "Christian" business?

> Have you been asked for a list of family or friends? If so, run – run fast. You are going to exploit your personal relationships for personal gain. This will... destroy many of your relationships.... Don't buy the lie that you are doing them a favor. This is just a way for you to rationalize the guilt you feel for using the relationship so you can get something you want.[3]
>
> (Dean, 58)

Diana and Joe were Amway distributors from New York who had their own web site for a period of time. This is what Diana says about their life after Amway.

The end of year 4, we sent a letter to our distributors with copies to our upline Directs. We advised everyone that we were taking a hiatus from the Amway Business. We advised our downline to contact their next active upline to place their orders and receive their books and tapes. We cancelled our voice mail, we cancelled everything. Since then we have been happier with the simplicity of our lives. We figure it will take two years and a lot of working overtime to pay off our $26,000 in debt. I guess it's a lesson learned.

Oh, by the way, we got a call from our Direct Distributor who couldn't figure out why we sent him a copy of the letter, he was upset because we didn't talk to him first. I guess he couldn't understand why we made a decision with our own minds… without giving him an opportunity to help us change it…. He said, "Hey, I thought we were friends?" I said, "Well if we are friends, than you'll understand right?" Somehow, I doubt he does. Or he envies us for having the guts to get out before we go bankrupt. He has never attained Profit Sharing Direct Distributor in the 7 years he's been in. And we have never attained anything higher than that one month at 1500pv. And we never will. Lesson learned…

Ok — it's been five months since Joe and I "gave notice" that we were quitting the business.

Have we heard from our upline? NO…

Have we received the money our downline shorted us on tapes? NO…

Joe and I have finally gotten our lives back. We have re-established the relationships we had lost with most of his family. We frequently have Sunday dinners at each others' houses, go to the movies or just hang out together. We are having so much fun! Of course, we are working extra hours at work, as much as we can to pay off the ridiculous debt we incurred as distributors, but still have time for our families and most importantly, each other.

My house is **clean** again!!!

We are going on our first Non-Function vacation in June and I am so happy. I still get twinges of nausea when I hear an Ama-term used in a sales commercial or if someone says something that was repeated over and over again on the tapes. But, in time, that will pass. We are not rich, we are not diamonds or millionaires, we are not financially "free" and yes, I don't like having to get up and go to work every day, but you know what? I am twice as happy now as I was when I was in Amway. I don't have to worry about making friends with people based on whether they do the business or not. I feel true freedom, to make our own decisions, to enjoy our lives as we please and most of all to have relationships with anyone we choose to.... "Ain't it great?"[4] (Brunjes, internet)

9. Have I found myself actually **avoiding** chances to meet new people since I joined the business?

10. When somebody disagrees with me about the Amway business, do I get angry?

If you answer *yes* to most of these questions, then you have been using your personal relationships. Sadly, a large number of people who join the Amway business do so initially because they see Amway as a way they can increase their income and make more of a contribution to charitable organizations and causes they believe in. Using personal relationships deceptively for our own ends creates high levels of anxiety, or **cognitive dissonance.**

Can I compare the "dreams" my upline talks about with how he actually spends his time and money? When I first got sponsored, I found this difficult to do because my upline simply wouldn't tell me anything about himself or his business.

Later, when working for my Diamond, I found some huge discrepancies. For example, he told me I would be able to give to charity and support ministries and causes I believe in. He talked about how great it was to be able to give generously. But as I discovered over a period of time, he himself gave almost nothing.

He talked about having financial freedom and control over his time. Did he

> Stick to your dreams and realistically put forth the energy and reachable goals for achievement... like [sic] we have done. You will feel better, be happier and have a whole lot of people you can truly call friends.[5]
>
> (e-mail)

[After studying the information my wife and I found on the internet], she and I started picking apart what had been happening to us for the last six months and it fell right into the pattern of a lot of the stories you have posted on your page. The feelings of guilt for not providing better for our children, driving 10 and 12 hours to a rally, never telling people what you are really doing, promoting books, tapes and functions, and, the worst of all, being advised to let our six year old figure out his own homework while we were out showing the plan and limiting his activities so as not to tie us down at home. We have really been questioning what we were doing for about the last month, and when we saw other people's stories and your page we finally, FINALLY, understood where the real money was being made. It made us sick. We are currently in the process of calling friends and family to apologize and alert them to what this "business" is all about.[6] (e-mail)

actually have financial freedom? Not that I could see! His entire lifestyle was financed. He didn't own his homes, his cars, his jewelry – it all belonged to the mortgage and credit card companies. Did he have control over his time? Not at all. He was working all the time. Usually he was traveling; when he was home it was almost always to **motivate** distributors by having them come to his house. If his own upline snapped their fingers, he was expected to jump to attention. It certainly didn't look like freedom to me!

Do I want the same "dreams" now that I did before I got involved?

Do I *really* want the material things my upline is showing me? Luxury homes and cars, expensive jewelry and the like? Were those my reasons for getting started? The answers to these questions were very painful to me.

When I got involved in Amway, I was very idealistic. I wanted to clean up the environment, I wanted to see that all people are treated with dignity, I wanted to provide a healthy and safe environment for my children, I wanted to give more to charity. But within the Amway business, I couldn't talk about my environmental concerns – fellow distributors would deride me for being a "tree hugger." I certainly couldn't become actively involved in any non-Amway groups – only a *loser* would waste his time joining the board of the homeowner's association, getting involved in an Earth Day cleanup project, or helping with a support group for learning-disabled kids!

Another set of questions you might ask yourself concerns your decisions outside of the business.

Does my upline try to control my non-business decisions?

For instance, does my upline routinely **counsel** me to come to him for advice about everyday decisions: small or large household purchases, my children's schooling, church involvement, employment, investment, finances, and my relationship with my husband or wife? If so, does he have any prior training or expertise in financial management, job counseling, relationship counseling, ministry, or business? How does he

A couple of months after leaving the business, a former distributor wrote:

[My husband] and I went to a party (non-Amway) around Christmastime. We knew only the couple who invited us. (A friend from his work). We both had a blast... met new people just because we wanted to... not because we wanted to prospect them. The next day [my husband] asked me if I found it refreshing to be around other people (people not in "the business")... I exclaimed a resounding YES. And that is when I started to realize how warped and onesided my life had become.

(After deciding to quit) my mom was very supportive and helped me make the best decision for myself. My mother in law said she's glad we finally came to our senses. (love her honesty).

I was at the mall today... was looking at all the people there... and was SO relieved not to have to contact someone. How bizarre, anyway. Blood sucker is an appropriate term. I never really liked myself when I was out contacting.... Now I like meeting people just because I think they're neat.[7] (e-mail)

We have gone back to our original plan of paying off our debt, buying land and building a house, and eventually buying a small hardware or grocery store. People in the Amway business say that if you go diamond that you will be your kids' heroes. Our kids, who are 16, 15, and 11 all say they are glad we are getting out of Amway. They tell my husband that they enjoy his being home every night. We could not be happier being out of the business.[8] (e-mail)

respond if I don't follow his counsel? Has he ever implied he would withhold business support if I do something without counseling first, or if I make a choice that's counter to his advice?

If I subscribe to Amvox or VoiceTel voice messaging, does my upline routinely send me political messages, or ever ask me to financially support a candidate outside of my district? Does he send me messages from Christian leaders, or recommend a specific church for me to attend or give money to? (This includes making financial contributions to the political or religious leaders he's invited to speak at the major functions.)

Has my upline ever compared the Amway business with God, Jesus, or political salvation for the country or the world?

Is the flow of ideas about building an Amway business a two-way, or a one-way street? By the time I joined Amway, I had been self-employed for about eight years. I had held board and committee chair positions in two different business organizations, and I was used to having my ideas heard. It was quite a shock to have my ideas about building an Amway business dismissed with no consideration. Instead, my upline just hushed me with comments like, "Gee, why do you want to reinvent the wheel?" "The trail has already been blazed, you just need to follow it. Wait until you go Direct (or Sapphire, Emerald or Diamond) to try out your own ideas. Your own ideas can cost you a lot of money."

If I was even mildly critical or had questions about the way business was handled, did my upline listen to my concerns and take action on them? No, he just told me things like, "you'll understand better when you go Direct (or Sapphire, Emerald or Diamond) "The more you grow, the more you'll agree" is a favorite phrase throughout the Yager organization.

But my upline certainly expected me to change what I was doing in response to his "suggestions." The implication was always present that if I didn't follow upline advice, attend functions, purchase SOT and BOM, my upline would no longer help me build my business. Throughout my Amway experience, I never felt that I was truly an "independent business owner."

The uncomfortable conclusion I finally reached was that I was involved in an organization that really didn't mesh with my values, goals, and ideals.

Do I Have Any Alternatives?

If you decide that being part of an AMO is not for you, you have another question to face: **If I decide to leave the Amway business, do I have any alternatives?** The AMO has been trying very hard to convince you that you don't. In fact, many people – I was one of them – actually become phobic about life "outside" the system. You originally looked at the opportunity because you wanted some additional income. While presenting the "opportunity," the marker man planted seeds of tremendous discontent with your current job and income, shot down most available alternatives, and dangled his business as the only realistic path to the success you were seeking. This message has been reinforced with every Introductory Seminar, Seminar and Rally, and major function you've attended, and every tape you've listened to.

I have my wife, kids, and my life back - that makes me a winner!!
Wanna know what 'real' and 'reality' is? It is having your marriage working and your house in order and your bills being paid, and being productive with your lives. No one in Amway is producing anything - they are nothing more than leaching consumer... consuming prospects along with their products. Distributors are not productive at all – it is all a house of cards – a re-routing of money. The worst part is this: For a few to make money, a large number of people must, as a rule, be losing money, and in lots of cases, losing big-time.[9] (e-mail)

Rest assured, there are **many** alternatives. First, remember that the "success" in the AMOs is largely illusory. The average Direct Distributor loses money every year, and fewer than 1% of all distributors reach even that level. The average losses of non-Directs range from about $4,000 – $6,000 per year. It's not hard to do better than that!

When I realized that in good conscience I had to leave the Amway business, I did not feel as if I had any alternatives. I realize now that I had become phobic about life outside the system, but at the time I was completely panicked. Despite my prior business experience, I no longer

Amway distributors are masters at putting down the "J-O-B" as a vehicle to financial freedom. However, an article in the *Cincinnatti Enquirer*, "Even P&G Rank and File Get Golden Handshakes" describes how "average" employees of the Procter & Gamble Corp. are retiring from fairly mundane jobs as millionaires. According to the July, 13, 1997 article,

> After 26 years working as an electrical technician for Procter & Gamble Co., David Perry retired last week with plans to sell his house and travel around the country for a year with his wife. He'll pack a cozy security blanket for the trip: more than $1 million worth of P&G stock....
>
> Mechanics, truck drivers, technicians and other blue-collar workers with the company 35 or more years could retire with as much as $750,000 these days - or more. And people in middle management or higher - even with fewer years at thecompany - are almost certain to leave their retirement parties knowing they are millionaires.[10] (Harrington and Bolton)

While Procter & Gamble offers a generous stock-based retirement plan, sensible financial planning can help you accomplish your retirement goals. Of course, sensible financial planning is not very glamorous. It's not as unusual, or exciting to retire at 65 as at 35, or 45. Neither does it require you to sacrifice your friends, your family, or your values.

believed I had any marketable skills. Slowly I came to realize that wasn't the case. But I had to take baby steps at first, stumbling along until I developed a little more confidence. Over a period of time, I came to believe that if my dreams were real, I could find a way besides Amway to accomplish them.

It takes **courage** to leave the AMO. Despite what you've heard on tape after tape, and at function after function, those who choose to walk away are **not** quitters or losers. I believe they are people who have recognized a dead end, deception, or fraud, and chosen to no longer participate. It takes guts to think about turning away from, or losing the love and respect of those you've trusted and confided in. Admitting that you made a mistake, or that you were deceived, is very difficult.

Income

Most former distributors notice an immediate improvement in their finances once they leave. They discover that the "Brand X" merchandise costs considerably less than the distributor prices they were paying for Amway-brand products, and see significant savings when they stop purchasing tapes, books and functions.

After the AMOs have put down your job and denigrated gainful employment in general, it is difficult to look again at a job as a realistic way to achieve your financial goals. However, the job you have is the best place to start. You might want to take a hard look at the career goals you had before you joined Amway. Maybe you need to dust them off and re-focus on them. Perhaps you need some new options instead. Two excellent books that might help you get started in your re-evaluation are *Finding Your Perfect Work* by Paul and Sarah Edwards, and *What Color Is Your Parachute* by Richard Nelson Bolles.

Possibly your Amway involvement has given you a taste for true self-employment. The numbers of self-employed people are rapidly escalating in the United States today, and contrary to what your upline probably told you, the average new business does not fail in the first five years. *Finding Your Perfect Work* can help you determine whether you are suited to self-employment, and will give you lots of ideas about possible businesses you can start. Another book by the Edwards, *Home Businesses You Can Buy*, discusses many businesses available today that can be

Just thought I would say "thanks" for putting up your page! I too, lost an 11-year marriage, house, and thousands [of dollars] being a "winner", being on the "10 steps to success", helping "other people to succeed", you know the mantra.... I am a single mother, but no chance of re-uniting with my ex (the man I left because he wasn't Diamond material) as he has since remarried to a girl who doesn't expect him to STP [show the plan] or listen to tapes or read books.... Unfortunately for me, I sacrificed the things in life that I really wanted, (a happy marriage, a modest but nice home, vacations with my spouse,etc) for what Amway and the "system" convinced me I HAD TO HAVE!!![11] (e-mail)

purchased and operated from your home. Your local community college, college or university might have some helpful courses or workshops.

Is it possible to fund a decent retirement from a traditional job or business? Absolutely! Some useful books might include: *The Millionaire Next Door* by Stanley and Danko; *Charles Schwab's Guide to Financial Independence: Simple Solutions for Busy People* by Charles R. Schwab; *The Only Investment Guide You'll Ever Need* by Andrew Tobias; or *You Have More Than You Think: The Motley Fool Guide to Investing What You Have*, by Tom and David Gardner.

Relationships

Can you restore the relationships that were sacrificed while you were involved with Amway? Probably. I was involved so heavily, for so long, that by the time I left I had no "pre-Amway" friends left. I hope that is not true for you. I am re-learning how to make friends. I'm the first to admit that it's not easy, after years of looking at people as "prospects" and only being interested in them if they could be of use to me in my business, but I'm finding it can be done.

I am very happy to say that I am closer now to my family than I had been for a very long time. They are extremely relieved that we have left the AMO, and more supportive than we deserve. Most of the former distributors I hear from tell me the same thing.

A young woman, who became involved through her boyfriend's family, wrote (names have been changed):

Situations became bizarre when Bill's parents fell out with their upline (daughter and husband in law) as Bill's parents claimed that their upline were stealing their downline (at this stage Bill's sister was at 21%). The result was that they have never spoken since, that was three years ago.

Bill's parents were very 'successful' as they were salespeople by trade and attained direct level. They began to have severe marital problems, partly due to the hours they spent appart and due to the fact that they felt they no longer had a daughter (they also lost a grandchild). The result now is the divorce of Bill's parents, a year and a half ago Bill's father was caught having an affair with one of his downline who was thirty five years his junior.

Today, Bill's sister is separated from her husband, but still partakes in the business. His parents are currently divorcing and the family firm is in a terrible state due to neglection. Bill's father was never 'thrown out' of the business on moral grounds. He excuses his 'life change' present divorce by claiming that if it hadn't been for the books and tapes, he never would have dreamed, if he had not dreamed, he would never have seen what else he could do with his life. Bill has lost a family and is now unemployed as he can't bear to work with his father in the family firm.

One of the saddest moments that I can recall from the past year, was Bill's mother sitting alone in her house, with the phone silent. That had never been the way before it was always constantly ringing with distrubutors. A month after her husband had left her, she never heard from her Amway 'friends' and all her old friends no longer called her as she had done as she was told and 'snubbed' them as they were 'negative'.

I can only express my feelings by saying that when I think of that business I feel sick and very embarrassed. I asked my friends and colleagues to see it, they might have ended up worse… what kind of friend does that make me?[12] (e-mail)

My Husband or Wife Doesn't See What I See

As a married couple, you join Amway with bright visions of a future where you can spend more time together and develop a closer relationship. Unfortunately, once you've plugged in, you have less time together, and the business usually becomes a source of contention – so much so that Yager's leaders warn you about "Ama-fights." What do you do if you've become disillusioned with the system but your spouse still sees whatever the upline has programmed him/her to see?

> It seems to me, by the statements they have made, that many of the leaders... really don't love people as they say; instead, they love themselves, and they love money. They are obsessed with money and what it can buy.[13] (Kerns, p. 118)

Ashley Wilkes decided to quit the business when he realized that his kids were getting more and more unhappy with their parents' constant absences, and when:

I just realized that I was losing my identity. I didn't want to. I'd given up all my identity, my critical thinking, and my personality.... The thing that makes me who I am. I felt like I was giving it up. The only reason why I guess I didn't decide before that was because [my wife] had told me that if I – at some point she had told me in the beginning – that if I didn't do it with her she'd find somebody that would.[14] (Wilkes, interview)

It was better for his children, but unfortunately it was the end of his marriage.

> *My kids didn't really realize the implications of it right away. . . but my extended family were very elated over it because they had all been alienated. My three brothers, my half sister, my parents, my cousins, they had all been alienated. I'd lost them as friends. So they were very elated when I told them that I was getting out. The kids were too young [ages 5, 12, and 13] at the time to realize the implications of it. But they did notice and appreciated the fact that I started being home, doing things with them again.*[15] (Wilkes, interview)

Four years later, Ashley Wilkes is divorced. Two of his three children live with him. Shortly after his divorce was final, he set up a web site titled *Amway Motivational Organizations: The Nightmare Builders* where he chronicles his own experience with *AMO-way*, as he calls it, and posts other information about the Amway business and its distributors.

Sadly, many distributors become estranged from their husbands or wives. Sometimes the damage can be repaired; sometimes not. This is one of the most unfortunate results of involvement in an AMO. Understanding the mind-control aspects of the AMO is critical to healing this relationship, and I recommend several books. These include Hassan's *Combatting Cult Mind Control*; Singer's *Cults In Our Midst*; and *Captive Hearts, Captive Minds: Freedom and Recovery from Cults and Other Abusive Relationships* by Madeleine Landau Tobias and Janja Lalich. You may also want to seek counseling with a professional who is familiar with cultic relationships. I wish there were an easy answer to this dilemma.

What To Expect After You Leave

What can you expect after leaving the AMO? Just as someone retiring from a job needs to plan some activities and anticipate possible problems in adjusting to the changes, someone leaving an AMO needs similar preparation. Here are a few things you might think about:

1. Realize that the AMO has taken up a lot of your time. What will you do with that time now?

2. Many distributors become motivational junkies or addicts. Have you become addicted to the tapes and functions? What will you do to supply your need for something positive and upbeat?

3. Originally you joined the business to make some extra money. After being involved for a while, chances are good that you need money now more than you did before! What can you do now to develop extra income?

4. You have probably spent a lot of time with your upline and downline distributors. Expect that once you quit the business, they will not associate with you any more. Can you re-establish relationships with family and friends, and spend some time with them now?

5. Your upline and downline "friends," those who convinced you that they were your "new family," may harass you or attempt to defame you in your community. How will you cope if this happens?

Whether marriages survive the Amway experience or not, there are some common aftermaths echoed in interview after interview, and e-mail after e-mail. Initially, feelings of anger, betrayal, or sadness will predominate. Here are some common observations from former distributors.

1. You feel stupid for being taken in so completely. This is because you trusted these people so completely, and because at function after function, and on tape after tape, they taught you to "blame the victim" (yourself).

2. You feel completely betrayed. You also have a problem from time to time trusting people, especially people who are being nice to you. You question eveyone's motives.

3. Making decisions may be very difficult.

4. You feel totally taken advantage of, or "mentally raped" as one former distributor expressed it. You are very, very angry!

5. You have trouble adapting in social situtations because you no longer relate to people outside of a contacting situation.

6. You have some impatience with other people, since you have been programmed to "just get it done" without questioning and you expect others to be the same way.

7. You feel like a complete failure, as if the whole AMO experience was all your fault.

8. You feel paranoid for a while. You may be afraid that someone is watching you. (One former distributor had the phone company send a representative out to check for wiretaps, and teach him how to check.)

These mixed emotions are a very normal part of withdrawing from any cult or other abusive relationship. Just as you must go through a process of grieving after a loved one dies, you must go through a process of emotional separation as well as an intellectual understanding after you leave the AMO. Most former distributors report that feelings of euphoria and happiness far outweigh the depression, grief or anxiety. Stephen Butterfield described leaving the business as "dumping an ugly master off your back."[16] (Butterfield, 177) Others have compared it to feeling a tremendous weight being lifted off, feeling lighter, or feeling that their lives have come back into focus.

After a short time, you may notice that:

- You feel an overwhelming sense of relief. The words "ordeal" and "nightmare" recur in your descriptions of your Amway involvement. You talk about "burdens" and "weights" no longer there. You experience a strong feeling of freedom.

- You are thrilled to be able to meet new people without that hidden agenda, and relate to them as people instead of prospects. You enjoy social activities again. You are happy to be able to tell people openly about yourself.

- Your upline – remember those people who professed to "love" and "care about" you? Who were your "family"? Don't expect to hear from them again. After convincing you to give up whatever family and friends you had before the business, and completely undermining your non-Amway social support system, they withdraw immediately, and – if you're lucky – completely. If they do call you, expect lots of anger.

- It's also quite possible that the same upline will begin a program of defamation against you. One distributor I was in contact with had to move across country before he was rid of their harassment. Others, who have traditional businesses, have been the victims of libel campaigns designed to harm their businesses or families.

- You consistently speak of being able to regain control of your finances and start getting yourselves out of debt once you leave the business. Those who did not go into debt are able to begin saving or investing again. You go on the first vacations you've had in years.

- You have more energy. You lose weight, or start an exercise program.

- You enjoy time with your children instead of rushing them around. When tucking the little ones into bed at night with a book, you don't fall asleep while you're reading to them. You find out a lot about your kids.

- Over a period of six months to two years, you go through a predictable process that is remarkably similar to grieving. You get angry. You cry. Sometimes you find yourself looking back nostalgically to the days when you had that safe-seeming Amway cocoon to wrap around yourself. Sometimes you find yourself "spacing out" or falling into unthinking, reflexive responses that you learned in the business. You may have difficulty concentrating, or learning new tasks for a while. This is probably not a good time to change jobs.

◆ Many of you will take all that energy you once used in your Amway business and do something entirely new: go back to school, start a new hobby, start a new traditional business, change careers, become active in civic groups. Some of you will try to put the experience behind you and move on to something else as quickly as possible. Others will choose to linger, using your experience to help others. Almost all of you will admit that you learned some good things from the business.

◆ You will re-examine your values and goals, and determine what's really important to *you* – not what some bejewelled speaker tells you is important to you.

◆ Many of you are amazed at the acceptance you get from former friends and relatives whom you've alienated because of the business, and relish the improved relationships.

◆ You find it helpful to educate yourself about what was done to you by the AMO.

Where Can I Find Help?

There is an ever-growing body of resources that can help you re-adjust to life outside the AMOs. Much of it is available on the internet, and we have included internet resources in the Bibliography. Since the internet is constantly changing, keep in mind that World Wide Web addresses and links may become outdated quickly. Because of this, we have established a website at http://www.mlmsurvivor.com where we will keep an updated listing of internet-based resources and current links. The Bibliography also lists books, pamphlets, and other print resources.

As financial and mental-health professionals become more familiar with the devastation that follows in the wake of many MLM opportunities, they are becoming better resources for helping people recover from AMO involvement. Your church or synagogue may have some suggestions, or may even have someone on staff who works with former cult members.

If you've read this far, I commend you. I commend you for:

* being open-minded enough to pick up this book in the first place,
* having the determination to read through a lot of information, which – if you've been a distributor – flies in the face of what your AMO has taught you, and
* your courage in facing the prospect of life outside the AMO.

I sincerely hope and pray that you reach the conclusions, and make the decisions, that are right for you and for your family. Here's to you!

Glossary

ABN	Amway Business Network
Ad Pack	A **generic** prospecting tape, and **generic** literature packed into a small manila envelope, and used as a handout when prospecting
After Meeting	The "meeting after the meeting," an informal get-together following an **Introductory Seminar.**
Amagram	The monthly magazine Amway publishes for distributors.
AMO	Short for **Amway Motivational Organization,** they are the distributor lines of sponsorship which participate in the system of books, tapes and functions.
AMO-speak	My word for the jargon of the Amway Motivational Oganizations.
Amvox	The proprietary voice messaging system offered by Amway to its distributors and their customers. The Amvox system can be *networked.* In other words, besides simply recording an outgoing message and incoming messages like an answering machine, the system can be used to send the same message to multiple recipients, and to pass along a message to one or more recipients. This system is widely used by US distributors as one of their major communication tools witthin each **AMO.** In Canada, the system is called **VoiceTel.**
Amway Business Compendium (ABC)	A collection of rules for Amway distributors. The **ABC** is included in the **Amway Business Kit.**

Amway Business Kit	The **kit**, which includes products and paperwork, that you buy to sign up as an Amway distributor. Formerly known as the *Sales & Product Kit.*
Amway Business Network	Amway's proprietary website for distributors only.
Amway Motivational Organization	A distributor **line of sponsorship** which has its own **system** of books, tapes and functions.
APRS	**Automatic Product Replenishment System**, also known as **ARP, Home Shopping Delivered**, or **HSD**.
ARP	See **APRS**.
Association	The word used by Amway distributors to describe proximity to one another. If you spend your time with your upline, that is a "positive" association.
Assumptive Attitude	Taking the position that your prospect will do what you want. If you **show the plan** with an assumptive attitude, you expect the prospect to sign up. If you promote a function with an assumptive attitude, you expect the distributor to buy tickets and attend.
Automatic Product Replenishment System (APRS)	A new **system** where distributors, and occasionally customers, will place a standing order for products. This order will be sent monthly, and billed to your major credit card.
Basics	The fundamental steps for building an Amway business.
Believe	To accept without question whatever your upline or AMO leaders say.
Believer	A distributor, usually **core**, who accepts everything said by his upline.
Book of the Month (BOM)	A book selected by your upline Diamond or other **AMO** leader for sale throughout the organization. Once you sign up for BOM, you cannot choose whether you want to take delivery of books on an individual basis.
Breaking the Kit	The act of sponsoring a new distributor. **Kit** refers to the **Amway Business Kit.**
BSM	Short for **Business Support Materials**.

Business Support Materials (BSM)	**Business Support Materials,** or **BSMs,** is Amway's name for the system of motivational books, audio and video tapes, functions, and certain communiction technologies sold by **AMO** leaders. The majority of income of the diamond-level distributors comes from sales of **BSMs** and not from Amway product sales.
Business Volume (BV)	**Business Volume,** or **BV,** is an arbitrary number assigned by Amway to each product or service. Along with **Point Value,** or **PV,** it determines a distributor's bonuses. (See Chapter 3.)
BV	Business Volume.
Challenge	AMO-speak for *problem.*
Cognitive Dissonance	**Cognitive dissonance** is the difference between a person's belief system and his actions. If you change a person's behavior, his thoughts and beliefs will change in an attempt to reduce the internal conflict, or dissonance.
Contact	Meet new people with the intention of enticing them to see the Amway Sales and Marketing Plan (the **Plan**).
Core	Indicates a distributor who is **plugged in** to the **system.** This distributor will purchase **Standing Order Tape, Book of the Month,** will attend all **functions** he qualifies for, and will purchase additional **tools** as recommended by his **upline.**
Crossline	A distributor not in your upline or downline. As a verb, it refers to communication with a crossline distributor.
Counsel	To seek advice from your **upline;** or, to give advice to your **downline.** This is not limited to advice about the Amway business; it encompasses advice about personal finances, marital relationships, childrearing, jobs, religion, politics, and any other life situation.
Crown	A level of distributor achievement. A **Crown Direct Distributor** has sponsored at least 18 qualified **DD** legs.
Crown Ambassador	A level of distributor achievement. A **Crown Ambassador Direct Distributor** has sponsored at least 20 qualified **DD legs.**
CV	The bonus value placed on **system tools.** These bonuses are kept secret from distributors until they reach the level of **Direct Distributor.**
DD	Short for **Direct Distributor.**

Deceptive Mind Control	See *Mind Control*.
Depth	A word used to describe the configuration of a distributor's **downline**. **Depth** refers to how many distributors are sponsored in a straight line from the first personally sponsored distributor.
Diamond	A level of distributor achievement. A **Diamond Direct Distributor** has sponsored at least six qualified **Direct Distributor (DD) legs**.
Diamond Club	Special meetings held by Amway for those who have achieved **Diamond Direct Distributor** status.
Direct Distributor (DD)	A level of distributor achievement. A **Direct Distributor** has achieved a level of 7500 **PV** in at least six months out of the fiscal year. If one leg of this distributorship accounts for 5000 **PV** or more, the distributor must have at least 2500 PV outside of that leg to qualify.
Direct Fulfillment	An arrangement where each distributor orders product directly from Amway, and receives his bonus directly from Amway. All foreign markets use the direct fulfillment system, and the North American market is gradually being converted. According to Amway spokesmen, this conversion will be complete no later than September 1, 1999.
Distributor	Any individual who purchases the Amway **Sales and Product Kit** and signs a Distributor Application.
Double Diamond	A level of distributor achievement. A **Double Diamond Direct Distributor** has sponsored at least twelve qualified **DD legs**.
Doublespeak	A term used by George Orwell in his book *1984*. The act of saying two or more contradictory things at the same time, and expecting both to be believed.
Doublethink	A term used by George Orwell in his book *1984*. The act of thinking two or more contradictory things at the same time, and believing both.
Downline	If you are a distributor, your **downline** includes those distributors you have personally sponsored, all the distributors they have personally sponsored, and so on *ad infinitum*.
Drawing Circles	Showing the Amway **Sales and Marketing Plan**.

Dream	The **rewards** you want from the **AMO system**. This may be completely different from what you thought you wanted before you got involved in Amway.
Dream Session	The most important part of the **Sales and Marketing Plan**, according to the **AMOs**. This is when the possible material rewards of the business are presented in a very compelling way, usually using a number of well rehearsed mind-control techniques to put the audience into a highly receptive trance state.
EDC	**Executive Diamond Direct Distributor.**
Emerald	A level of distributor achievement. An **Emerald Direct Distributor** has sponsored at least three qualified **DD legs**.
Emerald Club	A special meeting for those distributors at the **Emerald** level and above.
Encourage	The **AMO** word for *pressure*. For example, from your upline, "I strongly **encourage** you to attend this function." This means he is really going to put the emotional screws to you to pressure you to attend. After all, if you don't go to the function, you'll lose tens or hundreds of thousands of dollars, and be months behind in your business growth. Not to mention disappointing your spouse, and showing your true uncommitted loser colors to the rest of the **upline**. And if you don't attend, he will probably be too busy helping those distributors who followed his *advice* and won't have time to help you any more.
Executive Diamond (EDC)	A level of distributor achievement. An **Executive Diamond Direct Distributor** sponsors at least nine qualifed **DD legs**.
Faith	See *Believe*.
Fifty (50) PV Rule	In 1997, Amway changed the **Ten Customer Rule** to the 50 PV Rule. This rule states that, to be eligible to receive a Performance Bonus, a distributor must sell at least 50 PV in products or services to a retail customer(s). In February, 1999, Amway began issuing a disclaimer with bonus checks. (See endnotes.) (See also *Ten Customer Rule*.)
First Night Pack	A boxed collection of tapes, books and other materials that is given to a prospect for review when he first sees the **plan**.

FORM	A method for striking up what appears to be a spontaneous conversation based on mutual interest. It stands for *Family, Organization, Recreation* and *Money* or *Message*. If a distributor **FORMS** a prospect, it means he has begun a conversation and gotten some information about the prospect's family situation, work and/or hobby organizations, church affiliation if any, and then delivered a message relating to income or the business the distributor is involved in.
Friend	Anyone in your upline or downline. Publicly you profess to be very close to them. In reality, since you can't share anything negative downline (and neither can your upline) there is never the type of open communication that leads to real friendship.
Function	A **function** is a large **AMO**-sponsored meeting. These include **Seminar & Rally** and **major functions.**
Generalized Reality Orientation (GRO)	The *reality backdrop* that normally functioning individuals use in their daily lives. The **GRO** serves as a frame of reference for most experiences and activities.
Generic	Not mentioning Amway, products or selling. There are many **generic** tapes and pamphlets that are used while prospecting.
Goals	The stepping stones to achieving your **dream.**
GRO	**Generalized Reality Orientation.**
Group	The distributors in your **downline** comprise your **group.**
HSD	See **Automatic Product Replenishment System.**
Home Meeting	Showing the Amway **Sales and Marketing Plan** in a private home to a group of prospects.
Home Shopping Delivered (HSD)	See **Automatic Product Replenishment System.**
Honorarium	A hefty speaking fee paid to **Direct Distributors** and above for speaking at **Seminar & Rally** or at a **major function.**
Introductory Seminar	A presentation of the Amway **Sales and Marketing Plan** in a large group, public setting such as a hotel meeting room or restaurant meeting room.
Inviting	The act of inviting **prospects** to attend a presentation of the Amway **Sales and Marketing Plan.**
Job Mentality	A derogatory term for a prospect or distributor who doesn't see the *full potential* of the Amway business, or who actually expects to make money early on.

Kit	The **Amway Business Kit**, or **starter kit**, which contains the application to become an Amway distributor.
Leader	This can refer to a distributor who has achieved a certain **pin level**, or it can designate a distributor who is **plugged in** and doing what his **upline** tells him, regardless of actual accomplishment.
Leg	Each personally sponsored distributor starts a new **leg** in your organization. The leg will include the distributor you personally sponsor, the distributors he personally sponsors, all the distributors they personally sponsor, and so on *ad infinitum*.
Lifestyle	In AMO-speak, **lifestyle** means having lots of material possessions, including enormous homes, luxury cars, extensive travel, jewelry, furs, designer clothing, boats, airplanes and other toys. It also includes the so-called "freedom" that **Diamonds** have.
Line of Sponsorship	Can be very specific, as A sponsors B who sponsors C who sponsors D, etc.; or can refer to an **organization,** such as "the Yager **line of sponsorship.**"
Loser	Anyone who is not an Amway distributor, or a distributor who is not **plugged in** to the **system.**
Love Bombing	A tactic used by deceptive mind-control cults. As the name implies, **love bombing** involves a showy exhibition of interest and affection in someone for no reason that's apparent to the object of it. **Love bombing** gives prospects good feelings about the group, and strongly influences their decision to join.
Major Function	Large **AMO functions** held in major convention venues about four times each year. They have names like **Dream Night, Winter Conference, Family Reunion, Summer Conference, Diamond Rally, Go Diamond,** and **Free Enterprise Day.**
Making the List	Writing down the distributor's list of **prospects** who will be contacted and invited to see the Amway **Sales and Marketing Plan.**
Marker Man	The distributor who shows the Amway **Sales and Marketing Plan,** or **draws the circles.**
Mind Control	The gentle art of taking away an individual's freedom of thought by manipulating his belief system in subtle but damaging ways that are unrecognized by the individual.

MLM	See **Multilevel Marketing.**
Motivate	To elicit an emotional response from a prospect or distributor that makes them want to build the Amway business.
Motivated	Excited or turned on about the Amway business.
Multilevel Marketing (MLM)	A general term for business arrangements where the purchase of a distributorship also entitles you to sell distributorships, whose sales volume then becomes a part of your sales volume.
Naturalistic Trance Induction	A method of putting someone into a trance state through an indirect method of hypnosis, such as the careful use of language and method of speaking (pacing and leading) or guided imagery.
Negative	Any product not purchased through Amway or your **upline**; any information, including news, literature, art, music, personal opinion, television, radio, or internet sites which does not promote and support the Amway or **AMO** business.
Night Owl	A function, often held following an **Introductory Seminar**, for **core** distributors.
No Show	A **no show** can refer to either a person or an event. If you schedule a meeting to **show the plan**, and no prospects come, the meeting is a **no show.** If you schedule a one-on-one, and your prospect doesn't keep the appointment, he is a **no show.**
Nuts and Bolts	A function, often held following an **Introductory Seminar**, where **core** distributors learn the **basics** of building the business.
One-on-One	A presentation of the Amway **Sales and Marketing Plan** where an individual distributor or distributor couple **draws the circles** for an individual prospect or prospect couple.
Open	Introductory Seminar.
Open Meeting	Introductory Seminar
Organization	A distributor **line of sponsorship** or **AMO**. An **organization** can be huge, as in the "Britt Organization," or it can be small as in a new distributor's **organization** which may only be himself and one couple he sponsors.
Overcomer	Somebody who doesn't let his **challenges** stop him.

PaceSetter	An achievement level determined by the **AMO**. To qualify as a **PaceSetter,** the distributor would have to **show the plan** a specified minimum number of times per month, and sponsor a minimum number of new distributors. For example, the PaceSetter might be required to show the plan at least fifteen times each month, sponsor at least six new distributors personally, and sponsor another ten distributors **in depth** during a three-month time period. Some organizations use the term **Quick Silver** instead of PaceSetter.
Pacing and Leading	A speaking technique which uses the cadence and timing of language and voice inflection to induce a trance in audience members.
Pearl	A level of distributor achievement, formerly. This **pin** is no longer awarded, having been replaced by the **Sapphire** level. The **Pearl Direct Distributor** was a distributor who had sponsored three **legs** which all achieved 7500 **PV** in any one month.
Pearl Club	Special leadership meetings for **Pearl Direct Distributors.**
Personal Growth	AMO-speak for becoming indoctrinated. If you are **growing,** it means your thinking is agreeing with your AMO leaders'. If you don't agree, you need to **grow,** according to them.
Peter Island	A resort island in the Caribbean, owned by Amway. Diamond and higher-level achievers are sent on all-expense-paid junkets to **Peter Island** as part of their reward.
Pin Level	A level of achievement in business growth. **Pins** start at **1000 PV, 2500 PV, 4000 PV, Silver** (7500 PV), **Gold Producer** (7500 PV for three months), **Direct Distributor, Ruby** Direct Distributor (15,000 PV), **Sapphire** Direct Distributor, **Emerald** Direct Distributor, **Diamond** Direct Distributor, **Executive Diamond** Direct Distributor, **Double Diamond** Direct Distributor, **Triple Diamond** Direct Distributor, **Crown** Direct Distributor, and finally **Crown Ambassador** Direct Distributor.
Pin Recognition	A time set aside during a **Seminar & Rally** or a **major function** for distributors to be recognized for new achivements. Distributors are recognized for the **pin levels** mentioned above.
Plugged In	Same as core.

Point Value (PV)	An arbitrary number assigned by Amway to each product or service. Distributors qualify for bonuses based on their **PV**.
Positive	Anything relating to the Amway business or the **system**.
Positive Mental Attitude	Looking for the best in anything; expecting a favorable outcome to any event; ignoring any facts, feelings or information who don't help you to stay **positive**.
Prospect	Anyone over the age of 18 who is not an Amway distributor.
Put the Pedal to the Metal	Put more hours and money into building your Amway business.
Putting it Together	Building an Amway business.
PV	Point Value.
Quick Silver	See **PaceSetter**.
Quitter	Anyone who used to be an Amway distributor.
Quixtar	Amway's attempt to reinvent itself on the internet. Quixtar is scheduled to launch on September 1, 1999. Little information is available. It appears to be the Amway business, revised for internet commerce, and totally disassociated from the Amway name.
Reframe	To explain an experience in a way that manipulates the beliefs of the individual who had the experience. For example, when breathing exercises have caused hyperventilation to the point where the individual loses consciousness, the cult leader will **reframe** the experience as a great spiritual breakthrough.
Ruby	A level of distributor achievement. The distributor has a group volume of at least 15,000 **PV** in any single month.
Sapphire	A newly instituted pin level for distributors with at least two qualified DD legs.
Second Night Pack	Similar to the **First Night Pack**, but intended for review by a prospect after he's seen the **plan** and a follow-up plan.
Seminar & Rally	An **AMO function** usually held monthly, which combines **teaching** and **motivation**.
Service	To provide Amway products to a distributor not personally sponsored.

Servicing Direct	A **DD** who provides Amway products to a distributor not in his downline. This is done with the agreement of the upline DD of the distributor being serviced, and the **servicing direct** receives some compensation. This arrangement is used when someone is sponsored at a distance from his upline. Once all **organizations** have switched to **direct fulfillment**, these arrangements will no longer be necessary.
Seventy Percent (70%) Rule	Based largely on the existence of this rule, the FTC determined in 1979 that Amway was not an illegal pyramid scheme. This rule states that 70% of all goods and services are sold to retail customers. It was never, to my knowledge, enforced. Only 18% is really sold to consumers.
Sharp	A term of general approbation. A prospect or a new recruit is **sharp** if he agrees with the Amway program. If he doesn't agree, he's a **loser** or has **job mentality**.
Show the Circles	Present the Amway Sales and Marketing Plan.
Show the Plan	Present the Amway Sales and Marketing Plan.
Silver	A distributor who has reached a volume of at least 7500 PV at least once. Also referred to as **Silver Direct** or **Silver Producer**.
SOT	**Standing Order Tape.**
Spin the Circles	Present the Amway Sales and Marketing Plan.
Sponsor	As a verb, to recruit someone to become an Amway distributor; as a noun, the person who did the recruiting.
Sponsor Up	Sponsor a new distributor who is economically or professionally at your level or above.
Standing Order Tape (SOT)	The backbone of the **AMO** money machine. A distributor who agrees to receive **SOT** receives an audio tape each week, at a price ranging from $5.00 – 9.00.
Stinkin' Thinkin'	Any idea that is not **positive** about Amway or your AMO.
STP	**Show the Plan.**
Strong	A term of general approbation. Sometimes AMO-speak for *brutal*.
Success	High achievement in the Amway business, along with lots of conspicuous consumerism. In AMO terms, it doesn't matter how much you've achieved in the non-Amway world. If you don't wear a high-level Amway **pin**, you're not successful.

System	The **system** of motivational books, tapes and functions used and aggressively promoted by AMO leaders.
Tape of the Week (TOW)	The former name for **SOT**.
Teachable	A term of approbation to describe a distributor who does what his upline tells him.
Teaching	Whatever your AMO leader tells you.
Tearing it Up	A general phrase to **edify** a distributor. It implies that he is building an Amway business quickly; includes showing lots of plans or sponsoring lots of people.
Ten Customer Rule	A rule, on which the FTC based its 1979 decision that Amway was not an illegal pyramid scheme, which stated that Amway distributors must sell to 10 retail customers each month in order to receive a Performance Bonus. (See also *50 PV Rule*.)
Tools	The AMO system which includes audio and video tapes, books and functions, as well as certain communications technologies.
Trainable	See *teachable* above.
Training	See *teaching* above.
Triple Diamond	A level of distibutor achievement. A **Triple Diamond Direct Distributor** has sponsored at least 15 qualified DD legs.
Two-to-Five Year Plan	The *plan* for achieving **Diamond** status in two to five years. This is not a business plan in any conventional meaning of the word, and the average Diamond takes over nine years to achieve that level.
Upline	The distributor's sponsor, his sponsor's sponsor, and so on up to the *recognized* AMO leader. While there may be others who are actually part of the **upline**, they may not be recognized within the AMO system.
Video of the Month (VOM)	A standing order program for videos, similar to **BOM**.
Voice Rolling	See **Pacing and Leading.**
VOM	See **Video of the Month.**
Width	A word used to describe the configuration of a distributor's **downline**. Width refers to how many distributors are personally sponsored

| Whiner | Anyone who disagrees with or complains about the **system.** |
| Winner | A distributor or prospect who adheres to the **system** and is always **positive.** This has nothing to do with any measurable success. |

Bibliography

Amway Publications

Amway Corp. *Amway Business Review (SA4400)*, January, 1998.
———. *Amway Business Review (SA4400),* 1997 rev. 1998.
———. *Sponsoring* (TSA531H) , 1986.
———. *Intent To Continue* form, Sep. 1997.
———. *Sponsoring (TSA531H)*, 1986.
Amway Distributors Association. *Business Support Materials Arbitration Agreement.* Sep. 1997.

Books and Periodicals

Birmingham, Frederic A. "Rich DeVos: Faith and Family." *Saturday Evening Post*, Aug. 1982.
Butterfield, Stephen. *Amway: The Cult of Free Enterprise.* Boston: South End Press, 1985.
Chandran, Ramjee. "With Soap in their Hands and Hope in their Hearts." *Bangalore Magazine*, June 1998.
———. "The Amway Aftermath." *Bangalore Magazine*, July 1998.

Conn, Charles Paul (with Richard M. DeVos). *Believe!* Old Tappan, NJ: Fleming H. Revell.

———. *Making It Happen.* Old Tappan, NJ: Fleming H. Revell, 1981.

———. *Possible Dream, The.* New York: Berkley Books, 1977, 1978.

———. *Promises to Keep: The Amway Phenomenon and How It Works.* New York: GP Putnam's Sons, 1985.

———. *Uncommon Freedom, An.* New York: Berkley Books, 1982; Berkley edition, 1983.

———. *Winner's Circle, The.* New York: Berkley Books, 1979; Berkley edition, tenth printing, Sep. 1982.

Conway, Flo and Siegelman, Jim. *Snapping: America's Epidemic of Sudden Personality Change.* New York: Stillpoint Press. Second edition. 1978, 1979, 1995.

Dean, Athena. *All That Glitters Is Not God.* Mukilteo, WA: Wine Press Publishing, 1998.

———. *Consumed by Success: Reaching the Top and Finding God Wasn't There.* Mukilteo, WA: Wine Press Publishing. Third printing, revised and expanded, 1995, 1996.

DeVos, Rich. *Compassionate Capitalism: People Helping People Help Themselves.* New York: Penguin Books, 1993.

Edwards, Paul and Sarah. *Finding Your Perfect Work.* New York: Jeremy P. Tarcher/Putnam, 1996.

Edwards, Paul and Sarah. *Home Businesses You Can Buy.* New York: Jeremy P. Tarcher/Putnam, 1997.

Fitzpatrick, Robert L. and Reynolds, Joyce K. *False Profits.* Charlotte, NC: Herald Press, 1997.

Felps, Paula, "Inside scAmway." *Fort Worth Weekly*, 9-16 Jul. 1998.

Galanter, Mark. *Cults: Faith, Healing and Coercion.* New York: Oxford University Press, 1989.

Garland, Greg. "Amway: An Empire Built on Dreams." *Baton Rouge Advocate*, 26 Apr. 1998.

———. "FTC says Amway no pyramid but... " *Baton Rouge Advocate*, 26 Apr. 1998.

———. "Amway: Help comes at a price." *Baton Rouge Advocate*, 27 Apr. 1998.

———. "Britt System Successes." *Baton Rouge Advocate*, 27 Apr. 1998.

———. "Amway system facing court, image challenges." *Baton Rouge Advocate*, 28 Apr. 1998.

Harrington, Jeff and Bolton, Guy. "Even P&G Rank and File Get Golden Handshakes." *Cincinnatti Enquirer*, 13 July 1997.

Hassan, Steven. *Combatting Cult Mind Control.* Rochester, VT: Park St. Press, 1988, 1990.

Hedges, Burke. *Who Stole the American Dream?* Tampa, FL: International Network Training Institute, 1992.

———. *Who Stole the American Dream?* Charlotte, NC: InterNET Services Corp. InterNET edition, Dec. 1993.

InterNET Services Corp, *Profiles of Success.*

Kerns, Phil. *Fake It Til You Make It.* Carlton, OR: Victory Press, 1982.

Klebniov, Paul. "The Power of Positive Inspiration," *Forbes.* 9 Dec. 1991.

Liberto, Jennifer; Rothenburger, Aaron; Zebrowski, John; and Ziman, Jenna. "The Mother Jones 400: *Mother Jones'* third annual survey of the top 400 political donors." *Mother Jones*, December, 1998, pp. 49, 55.

Melton, G. Gordon. *Encyclopedic Handbook of Cults in America.* New York: Garland Publishing, 1986.

Mook, Bob, "Multilevel Mischief On Rise," *Denver Business Journal.* 8 Dec. 1997.

Morrill, Jim and Stancill, Nancy. "Amway the Yager Way." *Charlotte Observer*, 19 Mar. 1995.

———. "Yager Motivational Tapes Reel In Cash." *Charlotte Observer*, 20 Mar. 1995.

———. "Yager Puts Money Behind His Politics." *Charlotte Observer*, 21 Mar. 1995.

Poe, Richard. *Wave 3: The New Era in Network Marketing.* Rocklin, CA: Prima Publishing, 1995.

Random House, Inc. *Dictionary of the English Language.* New York: Random House, 1966, 1967.

Reynolds, Joyce K. "Multi-level Marketing: An Entrepreneu's Dream?" *Women's Business Journal*, Central Florida edition Vol. 3, No. 4, p. 14.

Singer, Margaret Thaler with Lilich, Janja, foreword by Lifton, Robert Jay. *Cults In Our Midst.* San Francisco: Jossey-Bass, 1995; first paperback edition, 1996.

Stancill, Nancy. "Life Within Amway: Two Views." *Charlotte Observer*, 20 Mar. 1995.

Stanley, Thomas J. and Danko, William D. *The Millionaire Next Door.* Atlanta: Longstreet Press, 1996.

Styler, Robert Morgan. *Spellbound: My Journey Through a Tangled Web of Success.* Fallbrook, CA: Sandy Creek Publishing, 1998.

Urquhart, John. "Amway, Canada Reach Settlement in Customs Dispute." *Wall Street Journal*, 25 Sep 1989, p. A5.

Vlasic, Bill with Regan, Mary Beth. "Amway II: The Kids Take Over." *Business Week,* 16 Feb., 1998, pp. 60-70.

Wolinsky, Stephen with Ryan, Margaret O. *Trances People Live.* Falls Village, CT: The Bramble Company, 1991.

Yager, Dexter and Ball, Ron. *Everything I Know at the Top I Learned at the Bottom.* Wheaton, IL: Tyndale House Publishers, 1991.

Yager, Dexter and Ball, Ron. *Mark of a Millionaire, The.* Wheaton, IL: Tyndale House Publishers, 1990.

Yager, Dexter with Ball, Ron. *Millionaire's Common Sense Approach to Wealth, A.* Charlotte, NC: Freedom Distributing Co., Inc., 1989.

Yager, Dexter and Ball, Ron. *Ordinary Men, Extraordinary Heroes.* Charlotte, NC: InterNET Services Corp., 1992.

Yager, Dexter with Ball, Ron. *Dynamic People Skills.* Charlotte, NC: InterNET Services Corp., 1997.

Yager, Dexter R., Sr., interview. "The CEO." *Success,* May, 1994, p. 18.

Yager, Dexter R., Sr. with Yager, Doyle. *The Business Handbook: A Guide To Building Your Own Successful Amway Business.* Charlotte, NC: InterNET Services Corp., USA, 1985.

Yarnell, Mark B. "Plunging in for Profits: Corporate America Joins the Revolution." *Success,* May, 1994, p. 20.

Zebrowski, John and Ziman, Jenna. "Tough Sell," *Mother Jones,* Dec. 1998, p. 56.

Legal Documents

Baker v Amway. State of MI, Kent Co. Circuit Court. Case No.: 91-72761-CK. 28 Jun 1991.

Cairns et al v. Amway et al, US District Court, Southern District of Ohio, 1984.

Federal Trade Commission. 93 F.T.C. 618. *Amway Corporation, Inc., et al. Final Order*. Docket 9023. 25 Mar. 1975. Final Order 8 May 1979.

Gommeringer v Amway. US District Court, Western District of MI, Southern Div. File No.: G85-832-CAl. 17 Aug. 1987.

Hanrahan et al vs. Britt, Yager and Amway et al. US District Court, Eastern District of PA. Civil Action No. 94-4615.

Heckart v. Britt, Yager, Amway et al. Superior Court, State of WA, Pence Co. No. 85 2 01841 4. 29 Mar. 1985.

Hart v Amway et al, US District Court, Middle District FL, Jacksonville Div. Case No. 97-349-CIV-J-20B. 8 Apr. 1997.

Hayden v DiSalvatore et al, Case #3:97CV1509JCH. US District Court, District of CT. 24 Jul 1997.

Morrison et al v Amway et al. District Court of Harris County, TX. January, 1997.

Musgrove v Amway et al. District Court of Harris Co., TX, 190 Judicial District. No. 98-17491. 22 Jun 1998.

NMPA v Amway et al. US District Court, Middle District of FL, Orlando Div. Oct. 1996.

Procter & Gamble v Amway. US District Court, District of UT, Northern Div. 29 Apr. 1996

Procter & Gamble v Amway. US District Court, District of TX, Southeastern Div., Houston. No. H-97-2384. 16 Jul. 1997.

Pruitt v Amway et al. District Court of Harris Co., TX, 190 Judicial District. No. 98-17491. 22 Jun 1998.

RIAA v Amway et al. US District Court, Middle District of FL, Orlando Div. Feb. 1996.

Setzer v. Amway Corporation, Richard M. Devos and Jay VanAndel, U.S. District Court, District of South Carolina, Greenville Division, 17 Jul 1986.

Shaffer v Talerico. City Court of Utica, Oneida Co. NY. 18 Feb. 1983.

State of Wisconsin v. Amway et al, Circuit Court, Milwaukee County, WI, Case No. 589806

Taylor v. Duncan, Amway et al. Superior Court, State of WA, King Co. NO. 98-2-15585-0 SEA. July 1998.

Touchton v. Yager, Amway et al, State of GA, Richmond Co. No. 96-RC5C-264. 28 Mar. 1996.

Miscellaneous

"Soap and Hope," *CBS 60 Minutes with Mike Wallace,* 1983.

Brooks, Douglas M. Written testimony to the Federal Trade Commission, 10 Aug. 1995.

Bryan, Tim; Fish, Tedd; Haugen, Randy; Howard, Greg; Wilson, Don. *The Basics of Contacting and Inviting (DBR474).* USA: InterNET Services Corp., no date. Audiotape.

Manzi, Jerry and Sandra. *Your People Are Your Family (PS77).* Private label series, distributed by InterNET Services Corp., no date. Audiotape.

Meadows, Jerry and Cherry. *Instill the Belief (SOT308).* Charlotte, NC: InterNET Services Corp., 1991. Audiotape.

Short, Bo. *It's Called Practice (GCS103).* Private label series, distributed by InterNET Services Corp., no date. Audiotape.

U.S. Department of Health and Human Serices, Social Security Administration, Office of the Actuary. *Disabled-Worker Projections OASDI Cost Estimates 1984, Actuarial Study No. 93.* Nov. 1984.

———. *Life Tables for the United States Social Security Area 1900-2080, Actuarial Study no. 107.* Aug. 1992.

———. Social Security Area Population Projections 1989. Actuarial Study no. 105. June, 1989.

Wilson, Don and Nancy. *Concepts, Principles and the System* (SOT 513). InterNET Services Corp. 1994. Audiotape .

Web Sites

American Family Foundation. *Information about Cults and Psychological Manipulation.* <http://www.csj.org>.

Anon. "A Different Gospel: J'Accuse!" <http://www.tc.umn.edu/nlhome/m307/wilke001/DiffGosp2.html>.

Anon. *Disenchanted Dreamers.* <http://members.aol.com/Viper0702/Disenchanted.html>.

Anon. *Dreamstealers.* <http://members.tripod.com/~dreamsteal/index.html>.

Anon. *Italian Amway Story, An.* <http://www.geocities.com/WallStreet/Floor/7361>.

Anon. *Multisense.* <http://members.aol.com/multisense/home.htm>.
Anon. *World Wide Scam Network, The.* <http://www.worldwidescam.
   com/>.
Barrett, Dr. Stephen. *Multilevel Marketing Project.* <http://www.
   quackwatch.com>.
Carter, Ruth. *MLM Survivors Homepage, The.* <http://members.tripod.
   com/~nomorescams>
Carroll, Robert Todd. "Amway." *Skeptic's Dictionary.* <http://dcn.da-
   vis.ca.us/%7Ebtcarrol/skeptic/amway.html>.
Crocker, Kelly. *Ex-Ambot's Web Page.* <http://www.angelfire.com/or/
   amwaydreamers/index.htm>.
FACTNet. Home Page. <http://www.factnet.org/>.
Gerard, David. *An Australian Anti-Amway Page.* <http://thingy.apana.
   org.au/~fun/amway>.
Glasser, Russel. *The Perils of Amway.* <http://www.willynet.com
   /rglasser/amway/index.html>.
Greenfield, Jason. *Amway: An Insider's Perspective.*
   <http://www-acc.scu.edu/~jgreenfield/amway_home.html>.
Groenveld, Jan. *Cult Awareness and Information Centre – Australia.*
   <http://student.uq.edu.au/~s101663/>.
Hassan, Steven. *Resource Center for Freedom of Mind.* <http://www.
   freedomofmind.com>.
Hoagland, John. *Welcome to Amway: The Continuing Story.*
   <http://www.cocs.com/jhoagland>.
Johnston, Ron. *Amway-UK Rip-Off.* <http://wkweb5.cableinet.co.uk/
   ronjohn_98/>.
Larsen, Scott. *Amway Distributor's Little White Lie, The.* <http://www.
   awod.com/gallery/rwav/slarsen/amway.htm>.l
Midgett, Charles. Other Side of the Plan, *The.* <http://www.tosp.
   cnchost.com/>.
National Fraud Information Center. Home Page. <http://www.
   fraud.org/>.
Probandt, Jeff. *An In-Depth Look at the Amway Business.*
   <http://209.196.24.186/>.
Roberts, Dave. *Ask-An-Emerald.* <http://209.110.55.90/>.
Ross, Rick. Home Page. <http://www.rickross.com>.
Schwartz, Sidney. *Amway: The Untold Story.* <http://www.
   teleport.com/~schwartz>.

Sommers, Pete. *Amway: A Very Bad Company.* <http://www-scf.usc. edu/~psommer/amway.html>.

VanDruff, Dean. *What's Wrong With Multi-Level Marketing?* <http://www.vandruff.com/mlm.html>.

Wilkes, Ashley. *Amway Motivational Organizations: The Nightmare Builders.* <http://www.tc.umn.edu/nlhome/m307/wilke001/ amway.html>.

Endnotes

ONE

1. John Urquhart, *Wall Street Journal*, 25 Sep. 1999.
2. Amway Corp., *Vision*, 5 Jan. 1998, <http://www.amway. com/vision.htm>.
3. Amway Corp., *Amway Business Review (SA4400)*, Jan. 1998.

TWO

1. E-mail to author, 24 Sep 1998.
2. Ashley Wilkes, a former distributor, interviewed by author, 9 Apr 1998.
3. Ibid.
4. Ibid.
5. Ibid.
6. Ibid.
7. Charles (not his real name), a former distributor. Interviewed by author on 25 Apr 1998.

8. Ibid.

9. Jason Greenfield, a former distributor, interviewed by author on 5 May, 1998.

10. Ibid.

11. Ibid.

12. Ibid.

13. As we go to press, we have just learned that in Feb. 1999, Amway for the first time included this disclaimer with distributors' monthly bonus checks:

> "Amway's Rules of Conduct require all distributors who receive a Performance Bonus to be in compliance with the Amway Rules of conduct, including the Retail Sales Rule and the 70% Rule. Acceptance of any Performance Bonus constitutes your affirmation of compliance with these rules. In order to assure compliance, your Direct Distributor may have your bonus paid directly to him or her for handling. If you have questions regarding this, please consult with your sponsor or upline Direct Distributor."

14. Greenfield, interview.

15. Roberta (not her real name) is a former distributor from Italy. She sent these comments in a series of e-mails to the author in the spring of 1998.

THREE

1. Conn, Charles Paul, *The Possible Dream* (New York: Berkley, 1997, rev. 30th printing Feb. 1982), pp. 22-23.

2. In April, 1998, the People's Republic of China put a stop to *all* direct selling in their country. Amway and two other US companies were later allowed to re-open, but all sales take place in retail outlets.

3. Amway Corp., *Amway Business Review (SA4400)* pamphlet, 1997 rev. 1998.

4. Amway Corp., *SA4400*, 1997.

5. Ibid.

6. Ibid.

7. Ibid.

8. Amway Corp., *Sponsoring (TSA531H)* brochure, 1986.

9. SA4400.

10. Ibid.

FOUR

1. Random House, *Dictionary of the English Language*, (New York: Random House, 1967), p. 1493.

2. Jim Morrill and Nancy Stancill, "Amway: The Yager Way," *Charlotte Observer*, 19 March 1995.

3. The People's Republic of China banned all direct selling on the mainland, effective April 21, 1998. They have since allowed three US companies, including Amway, to continue doing business on a retail-only basis. Amway China no longer has "distributors." Instead, there are "sales associates." All selling is done from Amway-owned retail outlets by sales associates. It may well be that Yager's InterNET and the other AMOs will be forced to pull out of China.

FIVE

1. Former distributor, e-mail to author.

2. Former distributor, series of e-mails to author.

3. Stancill and Morrill, 19 Mar 1995.

4. *Cairns et al v Amway et al*, US District Court, Southern District of OH, 1984.

5. ICCA, Intercontinental Communication Corp. of America, is the division of InterNET Services Corp. that records speeches, duplicates tapes, and has developed satellite TV programming.

6. Nancy Stancill and Jim Morrill, "Yager Motivational Tapes Reel In Cash," *Charlotte Observer*, 20 Mar 1995.

7. Robert L. FitzPatrick, co-author of *False Profits: Seeking Financial and Spiritual Deliverance in Multi-Level Marketing and Pyramid Schemes*, e-mail to author, 10 Apr 1999.

8. Amway Corp., *Intent To Continue* form, Sep 1997.

9. Amway Distributors Assoc., *Business Support Materials Arbitration Agreement* form, Sep 1997.

10. Former distributor, e-mail to author 27 Apr 1998.

11. Former distributor, e-mail to author 5 Apr 1998.

12. Jeff Probandt, "The System," *An In-Depth Look At The Amway Business*, 3 Mar 1998, <http://209.196.24.186/system.htm>.

SIX

1. There has been talk that InterNET would open all locations for Free Enterprise Days to distributors from any group. This would represent a major shift in policy.

SEVEN

1. Yager, p. 310.

EIGHT

1. As a distributor, you are taught that when a distributor you sponsor goes Direct, you receive an override bonus equal to 4% of that distributor's volume. However, because of some complicated rules, the reality is that most of that 4% goes to *your* upline Direct instead. As one former Direct wrote in an e-mail, "It's called leadership bonus override. It is one of the deceptive things about the SA4400 and what people show in the plan. Essentially, you have to give your upline a certain amount. When I called Amway to complain why that was so when we broke a Direct, they replied 'You have just experienced Leadership Bonus Shock.'

2. Probandt, "The System."

3. Morrison et al v Amway et al, US District Court, Harris Co., TX, Section V, Jan 1997.

4. Thomas J. Stanley and William D. Danko, *The Millionaire Next Door* (Atlanta: Longstreet Press, 1996), p. 12.

5. Stanley and Danko, pp. 8-11.

6. All figures are rounded to the nearest $1,000. The Diamonds brag about the size of the bonus checks they receive from Amway, going so far as to photocopy the big checks and distribute them through the organization. However, in any distribution business, the size of the gross income is not relevant information. What's important is the cost of running the business, and how much of that gross intake the distributor *keeps* after paying the expenses of running the business.

7. Probandt, "The System."

8. You will notice there is no category for Product Sales to Consumers. This is because, in a five-year period, this Diamond made only *two* product sales.

9. This information comes from the ICCA price list. If a company hired ICCA to duplicate a quantity of audio tapes for them, ICCA would charge 60 cents per tape. This figure already includes ICCA's profit.

10. Rick Ross, e-mail to author, 5 Dec 1998.

NINE

1. Jeanne Mills was a former member of the People's Temple who spoke out against Jim Jones' regime. She was assassinated a year following the November 18, 1978 Jonestown suicide/murders of 911 adults and children.

2. Steven Hassan, *Combatting Cult Mind Control* (Rochester, VT: Park Street Press, 1990), pp. 36-37.

3. Hassan, p. 40.

4. Robert Jay Lifton, foreword to Margaret Thaler Singer with Janja Lalich, *Cults In Our Midst* (San Francisco: Jossey-Bass, 1995), p. XII.

5. Ibid.

6. Margaret Thaler Singer with Janja Lalich, *Cults In Our Midst* (San Francisco: Jossey-Bass, 1995), pp. 5-6.

7. Singer, p. 7.

8. Hassan, p. 99. Hassan claims that "The basic feature of most cult recruitment is deception."

9. Hassan, p. 167.

10. Singer, p. 64.

11. Singer, pp. 64-67.

12. Groenveld, Jan, "Social Psychology and Group Dyanmics," Internet, 15 Sep 1998, <http://student.uq.edu.au/~py101663/general/totalism.htm>.

13. Ibid.

14. Singer, p. 13.

15. Singer, p. 17.

16. Hassan, pp. 43-44.

17. Flo Conway and Jim Siegelman, *Snapping* (New York: Stillpoint Press, 1995), pp. 92-93.

TEN

1. Singer, p. 57.

2. Singer, p. 60.

3. Hassan, p. 63.

4. Hassan, p. 65.

5. Conway and Siegelman, pp. 149-50. The emphasis is mine.

ELEVEN

1. Amway Corp., "Why do Amway meetings appear to some people like a cult?" Internet, 19 Feb 1998, <http://www.amway.com/question14.asp>.

2. Hassan, p. 56.

3. Hassan, pp. 99-100.

4. Mark Galanter, *Cults: Faith, Healing and Coercion* (New York: Oxford University Press, 1989), pp. 51-53.

5. Galanter, p. 52.

6. Galanter, p. 53.

7. Singer, p. 109. The emphasis is mine.

8. Panel, *The Basics of Contacting and Inviting (DBR474)*, audiotape (USA: InterNET Services Corp., n.d.).

9. Singer, p. 110.

10. Bo Short, *It's Called Practice (GCS103)*, private label series audiotape, n.p., distrib. InterNET Services Corp., n.d.).

11. Dexter R., Yager, Sr. with Doyle Yager, *The Business Handbook: A Guide To Building Your Own Successful Amway Business* (Charlotte, NC: InterNET Services Corp., USA, 1985.), p. 230.

12. Yager, p. 251.

13. DBR474.

14. Ibid.

15. Stephen Butterfield, *Amway: The Cult of Free Enterprise* (Boston: South End Press, 1985), p. 46.

16. Butterfield, pp. 48-49.

17. Yager, p. 275.

TWELVE

1. Dr. David Humphrey, "Dr. Dave's Organizational Open," transcript of audio recording, *Amway Motivational Organizations: The Nightmare Builders*, 16 May, 1998, <http://www.tc.umn.edu/nlhome/m307/wilke001/DaveOrgOpen.html>.

2. Ibid.

3. Jim Hayes, "Introductory Seminar," transcript of audio taping by author, Mar 1998.

4. Humphrey.

5. Ibid.

6. Ibid.

7. This is borne out by written testimony for the Federal Trade Commission from Attorney Douglas M. Brooks, who specializes in franchise and MLM law. In a response, dated August 10, 1995, to the FTC's question, "To what extent do purchasers of business opportunities obtain relevant and material information from the required disclosures?" Explain," Mr. Brooks responded:

   Formal disclosure documents similar to those required by the Rule [Trade Regulation Rule on Disclosure Requirements and Prohibitions Concerning Franchising and Business Opportunity Ventures, 16 CFR Part 436] are rarely provided to prospective distributors, and usually in compliance with orders issued in enforcement actions brought by the Commission or state attorney generals.... The marketing pitches generally include the following elements: ...

   ...The only investment 'required' to participate is the purchase of a 'distributor kit' or 'starter kit' at nominal cost, typically bewteen $35. and $100. The actual cost to participate, however, is often much greater.

8. Athena Dean, *All that Glitters Is Not God* (Mukilteo, WA: WinePress Publishing, 1998), pp. 71-2.

9. Don and Nancy Wilson, *Concepts, Principles and the System (SOT513)*, audiotape (Charlotte, NC: InterNET Services Corp.), 1994.

10. Jerry and Sandra Manzi, *Your People Are Your Family (PS77)*, audiotape.

11. Jerry and Cherry Meadows, *Instill the Belief (SOT308)*, audiotape (Charlotte, NC: InterNET Services Corp.), 1991.

12. Internet, post in "Guestbook," 27 April 1999 <http://members.tripod.com/~nomorescams>.

FOURTEEN

1. Butterfield, p. 177.

2. E-mail to author.

3. Dean, p. 58.

4. Diana Brunjes, *Diana and Joe's Place*, Internet, 1 Jan 1999, <http://members.tripod.com/~nomorescams/dbrunjes.htm>.

5. E-mail to author.

6. E-mail to author.

7. E-mail to author.

8. E-mail to author.

9. E-mail to author.

10. Jeff Harrington and Guy Bolton, "Even P&G Rank and File Get Golden Handsakes," *Cincinnatti Enquirer*, 13 Jul 1997.

11. E-mail to author.

12. E-mail to author.

13. Phil Kerns, *Fake It Til You Make It* (Carlton, OR: Victory Press, 1982), p. 118.

14. Ashley Wilkes, interviewed by author, 9 Apr 1998.

15. Ibid.

16. Butterfield, p. 117.

Index

O

one-on-one 28, 110
    def. 166
organization 133 - 134
    see *line of sponsorship* 2

P

PaceSetter 36, 67 - 68
    def. 167
pacing and leading 112
    def. 167
personal growth 31
    def. 167
plugged in
    see *core* 36
Point Value
    def. 168
    see *PV* 23
positive 52 - 54, 59 - 60, 117, 121 - 122, 129
    def. 168
    functions 55, 60
positive mental attitude 31, 59, 85, 153
    def. 168
prospect 134
PV 23 - 28, 33, 47, 69 - 70, 72 - 73
    def. 168
    rule 18, 163
    tools and 34, 41
    transfer 74

Q

qualify 1
Quick Silver
    def. see also *PaceSetter* 168

R

reframe 97 - 98
    def. 168

Additional copies of this book may be ordered by contacting

Backstreet Publishing
127 W. Fairbanks Ave.
PMB 409
Winter Park, FL 32789-4326
e-mail info@backstreet-publish.com